DECORATING WITH
FABRIC
LIBERTY
STYLE

CHARMIAN WATKINS

CONSULTANT EDITORS

OLIVER STEWART-LIBERTY
JOHN LAFLIN

EBURY PRESS
LONDON

CARE OF LIBERTY FURNISHING FABRICS

Do not use bleaching agents when cleaning or washing printed furnishing fabric. The possibility of shrinkage should also be considered when making loose covers and curtains and it is recommended that a shrinkage allowance of 5% should be made.

CHINTZ	Dry clean, or hand wash only (40°C/104°F). Do not twist or rub, and keep fabric flat. Rinse in warm water, drip dry, then iron with a medium iron whilst the fabric is still slightly damp, to retain the sheen which may be reduced by washing or dry cleaning. Do not spin dry. Chintz has been used in this book for upholstery. If you are expecting a particular item to have heavy wear, cotton or union will stand up better.
COTTONS	Dry clean, or hand wash only in 40°C/104°F warm water. Rinse in warm water, drip dry, then iron on the right side with a medium iron. Do not spin dry.
COTTON AND FLAX UNION	Dry cleaning only is recommended.
TANA LAWN (PIMA COTTON)	This is not classed as a furnishing fabric, but may be used in very lightweight articles as illustrated here. Hand wash in warm water (40°C/104°F) using soap powder rather than detergent. Most modern detergents contain optical brightening agents which, because of their whiter than white effect, can easily swamp the subtle colours of some of the prints, especially the commonly used cream background tints. Dry away from direct sunlight to avoid fading. Iron when still slightly damp.

Published by Ebury Press
Division of The National Magazine Company Ltd
Colquhoun House
27-37 Broadwick Street
London W1V 1FR

First impression 1987

ISBN 0 85223 595 X

Project Editor: Suzanne Webber
Editors: Penny Lane, Gillian Haslam
Art Director: Frank Phillips
Designer: William Mason
Photographer: Jon Bouchier
Stylist: Cathy Sinker
Step-by-step illustrations: Jane Cradock-Watson
Colour illustrations: Susan Robertson
Consultant for sewing projects: Sandy MacCaw
Researcher: Julia Wigg

Filmset by Advanced Filmsetters (Glasgow) Ltd
Printed and bound in Italy by Arti Grafiche Amilcare Pizzi S.p.A. Milan

CONTENTS

INTRODUCTION	6
COOL CHINTZ	8
MORECAMBE BAY	12
A RARE PANELLED BEDROOM	16
LE BUNGALOW	20
CAPRICCIO KITCHEN	23
SWEET PEAS	26
FEMININE DRESSING	30
BATHROOM SPLENDOUR	33
HOSHI	36
STANDEN	40
CONSERVATORY CHIC	44
DRINKS IN THE GARDEN	48
THE CHELSEA ARTS CLUB	51
ARTIST'S BEDROOM	55
ESSENCE OF THE ORIENT	58
COUNTRY PATCHWORK	62
TEENAGE STUDIO	66
ASCOT BOX	70
ALGONQUIN SUITE	73
COTTAGE SEWING ROOM	76
CONTEMPORARY KITCHEN	78
OAK PANELLED OFFICE	80
A BOY'S BEDROOM	82
MARBLED BATHROOM	84
BABY BLUES	86
THEATRICAL BACKDROP	88
EASTERN PROMISE	90
AN ATTIC WINDOW	92
SEWING PROJECTS	93
SEWING TECHNIQUES	139
INDEX	143

INTRODUCTION

*L*iberty prints have held a continuing fascination for woven and printed textile lovers since they were first produced in the latter part of the last century. They are particularly interesting in that they encapsulated several decorative movements developing at the time of the foundation of Liberty's shop in Regent Street, London and that they employed in their design some of the finest talents of the time.

One major creative movement was gaining impetus in England when Arthur Lasenby Liberty set up East India House in 1875: that of the Arts and Crafts. The Arts and Crafts movement took its inspiration from an idealized notion of medieval life, but there were other influences on decorative and design ideals as well. Oriental pieces had been filtering slowly through to Britain but with the lifting of all commercial restrictions between Japan, Britain and America after 1868, goods began flooding into Europe.

With three assistants, Arthur Liberty began selling oriental silks in glowing soft colours unlike any available in Europe. Instant success followed and within eighteen months he had expanded the shop to include many things oriental: vases, screens, embroidery, lacquer, Buddhas, Japanese gods, cloisonné enamel and much else. William Morris, Alma Tadema, Oscar Wilde, Rossetti and Burne-Jones were frequent visitors to the shop and it quickly became a fashionable meeting place with well-to-do customers queuing on occasion, waiting for consignments to be unpacked.

Having established reliable sources for oriental silks which were printed in England, Arthur Liberty persuaded British firms to experiment with eastern dyeing techniques and weaves. He set up in cooperation with dyers and printers Thomas Wardle of Leek, Staffordshire who were already working with William Morris, in order to develop the soft hues called 'Liberty Art Colours'. Textiles printed in these colours were sold in vast amounts for the delicate draping and festooning of interiors.

Edmund Littler's works at Merton Abbey, on the site of a pre-Reformation priory and later bought by Liberty, were used to produce most of the prints, the River Wandle having been in use since the mid-eighteenth century by silk and calico printers because of the soft quality of its water.

By 1890 Arthur Liberty felt the need for a new approach to design. Although enjoying great success with his oriental imports, Indian-inspired fabrics and interior decoration contracts, he had become involved in the Arts and Crafts movement with its abhorrence of extraneous decoration—'fitness for purpose' and 'truth to nature' and a loyalty to purer form being its maxims. Generally disliking many of the excesses of continental Art Nouveau, Liberty promulgated a return to a solid, simple craft ideal incorporating simply stylized plant and geometric decorative forms and Celtic images of the middle ages but, unlike the Arts and Crafts movement, he encouraged the use of machinery to make available this purified form of Art Nouveau to a wider market.

Several eminent artist-craftsmen were commissioned to develop Liberty's design ideal in furnishing fabric, Cymric silver and Tudric pewter ware, enamel and copper work, jewellery, Clutha glass and furniture, including Archibald Knox, Dr Christopher Dresser, Jessie M King, Olive Baker, Bernard Cuzner, John

Pearson and William de Morgan. Arthur Liberty formed lasting friendships with many of these designers and with them he achieved the definitive style that became known as The Liberty Style.

Arthur Liberty became a member of many influential societies and in 1913 received a knighthood for his services in the field of applied and decorative arts. It was not standard policy at that time to name designers and he was more concerned to develop a Liberty identity or image, but working for him on textile design during this period were Lindsay P Butterfield, C F A Voysey, Frank Miles, Arthur Wilcock, J M Doran, Edgar L Pattison, Arthur Willshaw and Sidney Mawson. During the 1920s and 30s many Liberty designs, still on sale today, were bought from the Silver Studios, the Peacock, Peony and Pheasant designs being bestsellers. Designers there included Arthur Silver, his sons Rex and Harry, and Harry Napper. Sidney Haward, who lived at Bedford Park, the first garden suburb of London, also contributed greatly towards the Liberty design style; a brilliant draughtsman, his work still holds good today.

By the mid 1950s block printing had become so expensive that it was decided to record all Liberty block designs on paper. Many of the original blocks were subsequently sold, but the traditional designs are still produced with variations in colour. However, while keeping its distinct identity, Liberty design has stayed abreast of the times and the company has shown a creative approach to marketing.

In 1958, for example, William Poole, fabric and colour design consultant at Liberty, had a collection of fabrics designed to coincide with the opening of the 1960 exhibition of Art Nouveau in New York. In 1966 an Art Deco exhibition in Paris was planned to include original Sonia Delaunay designs from 1925, so Bernard Nevill, who took over William Poole's place in 1962, planned new designs to match. Susan Collier, in the same position in 1972, felt a strong shift towards the 1930s and produced a 'Fauviste' inspired range of fabric designs. This tradition continues today under the direction of John Laflin with the consultancy help of set designer Richard Peduzzi, whose work includes the sets for Lulu and The Ring at Bayreuth and whose theatrical and operatic designs are exhibited at Gare d'Orsay in Paris.

Liberty has had an inestimable influence on British and European printed textile design since the shop's inception and continues to be unique in its championing of British designers. It is our wish to show you how these prints can be used for decorating in many different settings in the hope that they will inspire and provoke you to experiment. The rooms on the following pages have not been set up for the book; they are very much in use in lived-in homes. You will find instructions for making the various furnishings in the second part of the book, and I am sure the book as a whole will encourage you to make use of one of the most interesting collections of decorating fabric designs available today.

COOL CHINTZ

An Edwardian terraced house in the heart of London, with large, high-ceilinged rooms and well-proportioned windows, is an ideal setting for the elegant chintzes featured here. Oliver Stewart-Liberty, Managing Director of Liberty of London Prints Ltd, and his wife Catherine have lived in this house for two years with their two children, and wanted a change from the mixture of styles already in place.

The owners were anxious to keep the sand coloured carpet in their drawing room and to avoid repainting. Catherine Stewart-Liberty loves light coloured prints and wanted to emphasize the airiness of the room while creating a warm surrounding to its north east facing windows. With the help of John Laflin, design director of Liberty of London Prints, she chose an oriental flower print together with a coordinating stripe from the East India Collection.

The Madison print used for the cartridge pleat curtains, Austrian blinds and assorted cushions was inspired by Chinoiserie flower forms of the eighteenth century, and was re-introduced from an earlier collection of Liberty designs into the East India Collection, so called because the main store building in Regent Street used to be called East India House. The sophisticated stripe Capriccio, a glazed cotton which was designed specifically to complement all the oriental chintzes, is employed here to cover the sofa in the same shades of yellow, cream, soft green and grey-blue and gently emphasizes the soft buttery yellow of the walls.

A comfortable, larger sofa kept its original butter yellow covering, and this colour is reflected in the bound edges of the feminine, bowed tiebacks behind it.

A beautifully proportioned window is enhanced by a very pretty Austrian blind with matching cartridge pleat curtains suspended from a brass pole

Rosette trimmed tiebacks add interest to the curtains at French windows in the opposite corner, their bound edges picking up the warm yellow theme.

Ruffling at the base of the Austrian blind is repeated along ruffled edges of the cushions below it, and by the ruffled edge of the fitted tablecloth.

This is a gently relaxing drawing room, which Catherine Stewart-Liberty says has delighted all her friends. It is stylish without being over designed, and shows how a new environment can be created while retaining many of the room's original furnishings and paintwork.

Main scheme fabric

Madison from the East India Collection
Design no 1143005D, 135/138 cm (53/54 in) wide
100% cotton glazed chintz, pattern repeat 64 cm (25¼ in)

Capriccio from the East India Collection
Design no 1143004G, 135/138 cm (53/54 in) wide
100% cotton glazed chintz, pattern repeat 32 cm (12½ in)

Although Capriccio has been used here for loose covers, this fabric is only suitable for light domestic use.

------ ALTERNATIVE SCHEME ------
Trent from the Chesham II Collection, a William Morris design, gives a more traditional, though still light and airy, feel to the room.

Alternative scheme fabric for curtains, cushions and tiebacks only

Trent from the Chesham II Collection
Design no 1066010K, 135/138 cm (53/54 in) wide
100% cotton, pattern repeat 32 cm (12½ in)

Capriccio stripe has been used to cover this sofa, featuring the same shades as those picked out in the Madison print curtains behind it

A close-up view of the tieback and rosette holding back the curtains at the French windows, showing the plain glazed cotton centre of the rosette and the contrast binding of the tieback

Instructions

Curtains with locked-in lining (*see page 97*) with cartridge pleat heading (*see page 96*)

Stiffened tieback with contrast edging and rosette (*see page 108*)

Bow tieback with contrast lining and edging (*see page 107*)

Round fitted tablecloth with gathered skirt, piping and double ruffle (*see page 124*)

Lined Austrian blind with ruffle (*see page 112*)

Round box edged cushion cover with piping (*see page 120*)

Round cushion cover (*see page 118*) with double ruffle (*see page 142*)

Square cushion cover (*see page 117*) with double ruffle (*see page 142*)

Scroll-armed sofa cover with piping and kick-pleated skirt (*see page 113*)

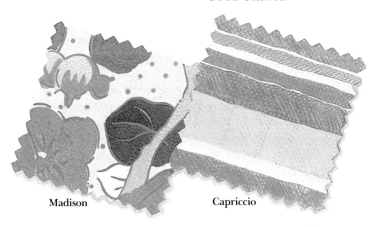

Madison   Capriccio

Trent

MORECAMBE BAY

An old rambling farmhouse, nestling in a small village set on the edge of Morecambe Bay in Lancashire, is at present being sensitively redecorated throughout by its present owners, a married couple. The area is one of outstanding natural beauty, wild and empty sand flats stretching away into the distance at low tide, and the mountains of the Lake District just fifteen minutes away by car.

They first moved to this peaceful and slightly forgotten area fifteen years ago, taking a cottage and then converting a barn. In the three-hundred-year-old farmhouse, set at the end of a lane with its orchard and gardens extending down to the sea, they have found an idyllic home. Spectacular views over the neighbouring National Trust farm to the sand flats beyond, the nearby bird sanctuary with its wild geese and resident herons, all contribute to the feeling of peace and country living.

The village, though small, is an active one, and in the local market and nearby auction rooms the owner does much of her antique collecting . Her husband is responsible for the printing of the Liberty wallpapers, so it was an obvious choice to make use of one of the prints in the bedroom shown here. Although the house itself is south facing, this high-ceilinged room is situated on the far corner of one of the extensions to the house, and needed to be warmed.

The choice of the turn-of-the-century Penelope print of foxgloves, butterflies and old English flowers from the Cotton Collection for both wallpaper and fabric has brought a warmer, prettier, and

Home dried and fresh flowers enhance the flowered wallpaper on walls and ceiling. The bedspreads were bought locally

more countrified feel to the room, emphasized by the view from the windows of the orchard, filled with aconites, crocuses, daffodils and many shades of bluebell every Spring.

Ruffles were added to soften the edges of curtains, tablecloths, chair and cushions. The plain binding matches the carpet and tones with the fabric and wallpaper. Two bunches of dried flowers purchased from the local antique shop augmented her own ongoing collection of home-grown flowers for a lovely finishing touch to the top of the cupboard, further enhancing the flowers on the fabric and wallpaper. She particularly loves to dry the tiny, old-fashioned roses which she says seem to be unobtainable nowadays, simply by cutting them just before full flower and hanging them upside-down in small bunches to dry out.

Main scheme fabric/wallpaper
Penelope from the Cotton Collection
   Design no 1063664A 135/138 cm (53/54 in) wide
   100% cotton, pattern repeat 54 cm (21¼ in)

(Right) **A short, circular tablecloth provides a very pretty covering for an antique folding table**

(Below) **The occasional brown in the Penelope print perfectly matches the rich brown of the corner cupboard**

—— ALTERNATIVE SCHEME ——
Santana from the East India Collection of Chintzes, a print adapted from a seventeenth century Edo period Japanese screen, gives a more elegant, less English country garden, feel to the room. The ceiling is left plain.

Alternative scheme fabric/ wallpaper
Santana from the East India Collection
   Design no 1143008C 135/138 cm (53/54 in) wide
   100% cotton glazed chintz, pattern repeat 64 cm (25¼ in)

Instructions
Ruffled curtains with sewn-in lining and contrast piping (*see page 97*)
Piped pelmet (cornice) with lined contrast-edged ruffle (*see page 106*)
Round tablecloth with bound and headed ruffle (*see page 124*)

MORECAMBE BAY

Penelope

Santana

A RARE PANELLED BEDROOM

When Jane and Jerry Scott, owners of an old manor house steeped in history, chose to redecorate their bedroom, it was with a design inspired by Chinoiserie flower forms of the eighteenth century on a deep, lacquer red background. The result is a spectacularly successful combination of oriental design and fine, seventeenth century craftsmanship.

The owner's ancestor, Sir John Fowler, a merchant from Islington in London, was responsible for the building of the manor house in 1637. It was sited on an estate in Kent passed on to him by Sir Martin Bowes, another ancestor, who had been granted it after the attainder or trial without jury and execution of the previous owner Thomas Cromwell, by Henry VIII in 1540. The manor house and its land continued to be passed down through the family to its present owners. Sir Martin Bowes was one of the family of goldsmiths from which the Queen Mother is descended.

The room featured here was originally a drawing room, situated on the east side of the house and was therefore a shady room within which to protect the very pale English skins so prized at that time. Although another drawing room still remains on the first floor of the house, primarily because of its views, this room has now been turned into a bedroom, its beautiful panelling being its predominant feature. The panelling is of Virginian pine which was first imported into

Madison is a successful foil to the rare, painted panelling of this seventeenth century Kent manor house

A nineteenth century embroidered Chinese chairback is draped imaginatively over a bedside table to tone with the Madison print bedcover. It is set with a ginger jar lamp in the same colourways

England in the seventeenth century. It is handpainted to resemble four different woods: cherry, walnut, rosewood and mahogany. It is a very rare piece of painted panelling of this period, a like example being found at the Victoria and Albert Museum in Kensington. A marbled wood fireplace stands opposite the ornate five-foot wide brass bedstead, together with an important walnut dresser and Chinese silk screen of river scenes.

Madison from the East India Collection was chosen to enhance the rich browns of the panelling, to tone with the existing carpet with its faded reds and to add an exotic oriental feel to the room. The Orient is further emphasized by the Chinese ginger jar lamps at each side of the bed, and by a nineteenth century embroidered Chinese chairback. The whole exudes a rich warmth which delights the owners.

Main scheme fabric

Madison from the East India Collection
Design no 1143005B, 135/138 cm (53/54 in) wide
100% cotton glazed chintz, pattern repeat 64 cm (25¼ in)

ALTERNATIVE SCHEME

Two different shades of Keswick from the East India Collection would make a radical alternative to the lacquer red shown in the picture, the dark colouring to be used for the bedcover and the paler background for curtains and valance (dust ruffle). The stylized arrangement of anemones, primulas, peonies and old-fashioned roses set on a background of japonica-like twigs, taken from an early nineteenth century chintz design, would form a complete contrast to the main scheme and create a restful atmosphere.

Alternative scheme fabric

Keswick from the East India Collection
Bedcover and tablecloth design no 1143007A, curtains and valance (dust ruffle) 1143007E, 135/138 cm (53/54 in) wide
100% cotton glazed chintz, pattern repeat 64 cm (25¼ in)

Instructions

Lined bedspread (*see page 125*)
Split valance (dust ruffle) with contrast-bordered top (*see page 129*)
Curtains with locked-in lining (*see page 97*) with cartridge pleat heading (*see page 96*)

Madison

Keswick

$\mathscr{L}$E $\mathscr{B}$UNGALOW

A turn-of-the-century English colonial bunga-low set within a glorious English country garden on the edge of the Seine at Mesnil-le-Roi is the setting for a celebration of one fabric, used to create a little piece of England in France.

The story of 'le Bungalow' is an interesting one. Madame Pauwels, once a comedy actress with the Jean Louis Barrault company, and her husband, a celebrated novelist and editor of *Le Figaro* magazine and *Madame Figaro*, have lived here happily for over thirty years. Her grandfather, having married an Englishwoman and wishing to make her more at home in France, purchased the bungalow in prefabricated form in 1905, from the firm of Boulton and Paul in Norwich. Its pine and thatch construction was shipped back to France where it is now set on a gentle incline overlooking a panoramic view of meadows, amid a beautiful and extensive garden containing many English plant varieties.

Wishing to extend the garden into the house, Madame Pauwels was immediately delighted with the soft honeysuckle blues and muted leafy greens of this William Morris design, not least because it was also very much in period with the bungalow and its furniture, and English style. The Arts and Crafts Movement so strongly championed by Morris made much of the nostalgic 'back to nature' ideal of innocent rustic living.

The backgrounds of Morris's designs were often dark and heavy, which although fashionable for that period, needed lifting and lightening for wider appeal. This Liberty did, and the soft

light browns of the Honeysuckle design from the Cotton Collection proved a perfect match for the mid browns of the 1880s bamboo furniture. It complemented the darker brown walls and reflected, to Madame Pauwels' particular delight, the muted earthy brown of the existing carpet. Here she has made full use of the fabric for curtains, lampshades, upholstery, tablecloth, box and scatter cushions.

Main scheme fabric

Honeysuckle from the Cotton Collection
Design no 1069681E, 135/138 cm (53/54 in) wide
100% cotton, pattern repeat 51 cm (20 in)

——— ALTERNATIVE SCHEME ———

The alternative fabric Lodden from the Chesham Collection is similar in style and period, but would create a lighter, more summery feel within a rather dark room. Here the print would be used for curtains, chairs and lampshade, together with a plain cream cotton glazed chintz tablecloth.

Alternative scheme fabric

Lodden from the Chesham Collection
Design no 1069622B, 135/138 cm (53/54 in) wide
100% cotton, pattern repeat 49 cm (19¼ in)
Plain 100% cotton glazed chintz, design no 1150001M, 135/138 cm (53/54 in) wide

Instructions

Curtains with locked-in lining (*see page 97*) with cartridge pleat heading (*see page 96*)
Simple rectangular tablecloth (*see page 124*)
Rectangular box edged cushion cover with piping (*see page 119*)
Rectangular cushion (*see page 117*) with piping (*see page 141*)

Alternative scheme illustrated overleaf

A William Morris design in soft blues, leafy greens and light browns emphasizes the soft, earthy browns of the carpet and darker walls, while providing a near perfect period match with an early prefabricated English bungalow in a French setting

Honeysuckle

Alternative scheme for Le Bungalow

Lodden

CAPRICCIO KITCHEN

A town house in London is the setting for the versatile and countrified kitchen, which to the owner Sandy MacCaw is the focal point of the house. As a self-employed person running two businesses from her home, she is more aware than most of the importance of her domestic surroundings and of the need for space and light.

When Sandy bought her house thirteen years ago, the kitchen was decorated a cheap and cheerful orange. Her criteria were that it should be a pleasant and comfortable eating place, somewhere to sit with friends, but that it should double at times as a work area. Sandy runs a successful soft furnishings business, working mainly for private clients decorating their homes. While concentrating on heavy silks used as an increasingly fantasy style of decoration, she believes firmly that soft furnishings should form the background for lovely objects or paintings.

In time the orange kitchen palled and a neutral background was chosen against which colour could glow. A café feel was envisaged, so natural pine units were fitted with white tiled work-surfaces

A richly ruffled and striped Austrian blind with contrasting apple green binding matches the Capriccio stripe of the ruffled valance to bring life and warmth to a town house kitchen

A luxuriously gathered Austrian blind softens the line of kitchen door and window, the green of the Capriccio print, its contrast piping and binding emphasizing the foliage beyond

interspersed with white handmade tiles in relief patterns of fruit and flowers, as were the white tiled walls. The use of Capriccio cotton glazed chintz from the East India Collection, with its marvellous striped shades of apple green, tomato, tangerine, china blue and grey on a cream ground, was chosen to liven up natural pine, the tomato giving warmth to what could be a cold and dark-looking kitchen, the green leading the eye outwards towards a patio filled with pots of flowers and greenery. The purchase of red pots and pans to echo the red of blinds has proved a very simple and successful way of pulling together the look of the room. The ruffled valance provides a soft contrast to the hard angles of the surrounding units.

Main scheme fabric
Capriccio from the East India Collection
   Design no 1143004F, 135/138 cm (53/54 in) wide
   100% cotton glazed chintz, vertical stripe, pattern repeat 32 cm (12½ in)

ALTERNATIVE SCHEME
In Hedgerow from the Chesham II Collection, originally a Sixties design and one of the few Liberty prints on a white background, fruits and berries emphasize the country feel of the kitchen, complementing the relief patterned tiles on the walls.

Alternative scheme fabric
Hedgerow from the Chesham II Collection
   Design no 1066014F, 135/138 cm (53/54 in) wide
   100% cotton, 64 cm (25¼ in) half drop repeat

Instructions
Unlined Austrian blind (*see page 111*)
Curved valance with ruffled piped edge (*see page 100*)

Capriccio

Hedgerow

*S*WEET *P*EAS

When Victoria Sykes visited the home of John Laflin, Design Director of Liberty of London Prints Ltd, and saw the sponged walls, she immediately wanted to update her own bedroom in the same way. Since her bed and its coverings were beginning to look a little scruffy, it was obvious that they also had to be changed.

The seventeen-year-old daughter of Valerie Goad (who runs a thriving business designing children's clothes using Liberty Tana lawns extensively), Victoria is an extremely vital, erudite teenager with an avid interest in the arts.

The bedroom was sponged by Victoria in pink and blue on a white background using small, natural sponges and the finished effect delighted her: 'like waking up each morning in pink and white clouds,' she says. The very pretty and sophisticated Sweet Pea design on a creamy white ground, from an original drawing by the flower artist and textile designer Sidney Haward, was chosen to tone with the walls. Haward, who owned a garden full of flowers and worked closely with Liberty in the years around the turn of the century, produced many successful designs for the firm.

The print was used to cover both head- and footboards of a lovely old bed which had been given to Victoria by her grandmother five years previously, as well as for the scalloped fitted bedcover, split-cornered valance (dust ruffle) and washstand curtain. Her aunt helped her in the re-covering of the bed boards, which were already well padded, the Sweet Pea fabric being stretched evenly across the existing chintz. Tiny ornamental boxes from her collection are

The turn-of-the-century design Sweet Pea by Sidney Haward proves the perfect choice for a seventeen-year-old's bedroom

Delicate bamboo
furniture perfectly
complements the Sweet
Pea fabric used for the
washstand and window
curtains, while a picture
of Victoria Sykes' twin
sister, photographed by
Snowdon, takes pride of
place on the little table

arranged on the bookshelf together with
old scent bottles from the 1920s.
Victoria, like her mother, who collects
Clarice Cliff ceramics from the 1930s,
loves a bargain, and the occasional
rummage in the family furniture store
produces alternative pieces of furniture.

Main scheme fabric
Sweet Pea from the Cotton Collection
   Design no 1061613B, 135/138 cm (53/54 in)
   wide
   100% cotton, pattern repeat 64 cm ($25\frac{1}{4}$ in)

────── ALTERNATIVE SCHEME ──────
The busier more cottage print Briarwood, also from the Cotton Collection, a
design of dog roses, violets and birds in
the William Morris style, could be chosen
as a contrast to the more sophisticated
Sweet Pea.

Alternative scheme fabric
Briarwood from the Cotton Collection
   Design no 1069674A, 135/138 cm (53/54 in)
   wide
   100% cotton, pattern repeat 20 cm (8 in)

Instructions
**Re-covering head- and footboards (*see
   page 138*)**
**Lined fitted bedspread with pillow gussets
   and scalloped edge (*see page 126*)**
**Split valance (dust ruffle) with contrast-
   bordered top (*see page 129*)**
**Square cushion (*see page 118*) with knife-
   pleated ruffle (*see page 142*)**

Sweet Pea

Briarwood

FEMININE DRESSING

Valerie Goad lives with her husband Mark and their five children in a lovely old red brick Kent farmhouse near Sevenoaks, from which they run a children's design and clothing company which makes good use of the Tana lawns so recognizable as Liberty's for their tiny sprig, flower and geometric designs.

Their bedroom contains quite beautiful French Provincial furniture from the late eighteenth and early nineteenth centuries, collected by his family in Wiltshire about forty years ago. The chest of drawers features many different birds including beautifully inlaid mother-of-pearl storks in full flight, peacocks, water fowl and birds of prey set round with roses, peonies, the branches of fir trees and other vegetation.

Handpainted roses, hollyhocks and fuchsia are among the varieties found in a design of flowers in an ornate vase at the centre of the bedhead, while gold scrolling picks out the shaped top and base of the headboard. In choosing a covering for such a bed, Valerie Goad decided upon the palest shades of Liberty Tana lawns which were made up by her old nannie into a diagonally stitched and quilted bedspread to give a very feminine but traditional look, which enhances rather than detracts from the ornate furniture. Five classic print designs were chosen which were used on their wrong sides to produce a more faded antique look to the covering.

Antique lace was gathered in layers to make flounces around the base of the bed, while ruffled antique lace cushions were piled at its head. Softly draped lace curtains, held in place with creamy-white satin ribbons, complete an overtly feminine and pretty bedroom of great style.

Main scheme fabric
A selection of classic Tana lawns
90 cm (35 in) wide
100% cotton lawn

Softly faded shades of
Tana lawns enhance
superb French Provincial
furniture of the late
eighteenth and early
nineteenth centuries

—— ALTERNATIVE SCHEME ——
Opium from the East India Collection
makes a complete contrast to the Tana
lawns, a design of golden dragons on
black background with lacquer red
border taken from a Coromandel incised
lacquer screen design of the late seventeenth century. The colours match those
of the ornate French bed. This fabric
would be better made up into a simple
throwover bedspread, rather than quilted.

Alternative scheme fabric
Opium from the East India Collection
    Design no 1143002A, 135/138 cm (53/54 in)
    wide
    100% cotton glazed chintz, pattern repeat
    64 cm ($25\frac{1}{4}$ in)

Instructions
Patchwork bedspread with diagonal
    quilting (*see page 127*)
Alternative scheme illustrated overleaf

Opium

Alternative scheme for Feminine Dressing

BATHROOM SPLENDOUR

A warm cosy bathroom in shades of blue and filled with paintings, antique furniture and interesting objects was the image the owner had in mind when choosing a new print for curtains, valance and blinds.

Liz Stewart-Liberty and her husband share a mock Tudor Buckinghamshire house dating from 1913, when it was built as a wedding present for her in-laws. With its 'joke-oak' design it has been lived in by her husband's family since it was built, so it is very much a family home. 'I hope it is welcoming, warm, pretty and comfortable,' she said. 'Everything in it has a meaning for my husband and myself, having been inherited or collected over a number of years. I should like to think that all the bits and pieces hang together to give an impression of a comfortable jumble.'

Colour, warmth and masses of flowers

are her 'worst and most serious indulgence'. She is a talented painter of flowers, butterflies and birds, with a finely developed sense of colour and a free and semi-abstract style. Having already had three shows in as many years of painting, she works almost every day in one of the bedrooms. Her husband also has an office at home. In this change of curtains and blinds she broke with the household tradition of light-coloured prints and plumped immediately for Bladon from the East India Collection on a dark blue background, which tones perfectly with the blue walls and carpet. Her one decorating maxim is that one strong pattern is enough in a room and that fabric should be cheap and luxuriously full rather than expensive and skimpy.

The dark blues, reds and peach colourings of this Bladon design, adapted from a late nineteenth century design which shows both Indian calico print and Chinoiserie influence, matches the nearby comfortable sofa. The tiebacks and valance are bound in a coordinating red glazed cotton. Original wrought iron finials and square curtain rail have been retained and the curtains are fixed, their floor length adding a living room feel to the room and the Roman blind providing privacy.

In a perfect world, Liz Stewart-Liberty says, she would like to think that her house reflected her personality, and was a welcoming place to return for warmth, comfort and pleasure. This bathroom certainly fulfils her wish.

Main scheme fabric
Bladon from the East India Collection
  Design no 1143003B, 135/138 cm (53/54 in) wide
  100% cotton glazed chintz, pattern repeat 64 cm (25¼ in) half drop

The design of a decorative white-painted wrought iron finial is echoed in the bamboo leaf detail of the oriental print Bladon

Bladon is gathered into contrast-bound tiebacks by silky cord threaded through buttonhole openings

—— ALTERNATIVE SCHEME ——
Mariana, a strongly stylized print of Empire feel adapted from a seventeenth century silk damask in shades of mid blue, red and peach gives a lighter, fresher look which also matches the blues and reds of the room.

Alternative scheme fabric
Mariana from the East India Collection
  Design no 1143009B, 135/138 cm (53/54 in) wide
  100% cotton glazed chintz, pattern repeat 64 cm (25¼ in)

Instructions
Roman blind (*see page 109*)
Combined curtain and valance (*see page 100*)
Lined tieback with cord and contrast edging (*see page 107*)

Luxuriously gathered curtains, valance and tiebacks create a warm and welcoming room in which antique furniture, objects and the owner's own paintings are found in happy combination

Bladon

Mariana

HOSHI

The Salcombe Estuary stretching from Kings-bridge to Salcombe bar is the home of the very beautiful and prized Hoshi, a 1909 gaff-rigged schooner of 25 metres (72 feet), with a heavy bowsprit, which has been owned since 1952 by the Island Cruising Club. The estuary is one of the finest in Britain for both high and low tide sailing, and the surrounding coastline, stretching past the Devon cliffs to Cornwall, makes glorious viewing from the sea.

Hoshi was built by Camper and Nicholson in Gosport as a private yacht for a Scot by the name of J Oswald. She is a classic Edwardian sailing ship that continues to win many important international races, amongst them the 1970 Tall Ships Race to Lisbon with an all-female crew. Her frame is of oak, her hull a Honduras mahogany, the deck is teak and the mast and boom are pine. She was rebuilt, rigged and decked in the original woods in 1933. Although her sails used to be of cotton, harder wearing terylene sails now replace them which last up to seven years.

A vinyl coated piped box edged cushion in Salazar print, with lockers behind and below, doubles as a single berth down one side of the main saloon

(Far right) The main saloon of mahogany, oak and pine showing the bunk base in its resting position as a seat back. On the table sit a chart of Port St Malo and approaches, brass and steel dividers, parallel rules, binoculars and skipper's watch while on the shelf behind rest a brass fog horn and hand-held compass. The wooden door knob is carved in the shape of a rope knot, while the plaques on the wall are for international races won between 1964 and 1984

to Gothenburg. STA rules demand that at least fifty per cent of the crew be under the age of twenty-five, so the opportunity for younger people is tremendous. She returns home by way of the Orkneys and the Isle of Man, taking in many beautiful and unspoilt Irish harbours.

Because of the high percentage of young people working the ship, the fresh young Salazar design, with a tough vinyl coating, from the Chesham II Collection, was chosen for both the cushions and the bunk bed base in the main saloon. The vinyl coating of the print was absolutely essential given that the saloon and its occupants are very often damp; ordinary cotton covers would soon be rotted by sea water. Salazar was chosen especially since it is a modern design compatible in colour to the interior, yet its broken stripe will suit any period. Here it blends beautifully with the mahogany panelling, oak beams and pine floor, adding a masculine modern feel to the saloon.

Main scheme fabric
Salazar from the Chesham II Collection
  Design no 1066003A, 135/138 cm (53/54 in) wide
  100% cotton, vinyl coated to order at Liberty, pattern repeat 32 cm (12½ in)

—— ALTERNATIVE SCHEME ——
Clementina from the Chesham II Collection, an 1890s design from the Liberty archives, is a period match with the schooner. It gives a more ornate sophisticated feel to the main saloon and complements the mahogany brown of the panelling.

Alternative scheme fabric
Clementina from the Chesham II Collection
  Design no 1066013N, 135/138 cm (53/54 in) wide
  100% cotton, pattern repeat 27 cm (10½ in)

Instructions
Rectangular box edged cushion with piping
  (*see page 119*)
Bunk cover (*see page 122*)

The 1909 gaff-rigged schooner Hoshi in full sail, a glorious sight on a summer's day

The Island Cruising Club, with a fleet of nearly one hundred yachts and day boats, runs cruises on Hoshi with a permanent crew of qualified skipper, mate and cook together with a crew of nine from the age of fifteen upwards, who cover both watches and washing up. Her sailing season lasts from May to October and she completes many one-week, cross-Channel cruises taking in the Channel Islands and Brittany, whilst some 10-day and fortnight cruises range further afield.

During July and August of each year Hoshi enters the Sail Training Association's Tall Ships Race, cruising up to the starting point at Larvik, situated at the entrance to the Oslo fiord, and racing

Salazar

Clementina

$\mathscr{S}$ TANDEN

Standen is one of the few Victorian houses owned by the National Trust, and is situated just south of East Grinstead in West Sussex. It was based on a collection of primarily medieval farm buildings and was designed by the architect Philip Webb (1831–1915) for James Beale, a successful solicitor, and his family as an unpretentious and comfortable country retreat for weekends, holidays and for their eventual retirement.

$\mathscr{P}$hilip Webb was a lifelong friend of William Morris, the champion of nineteenth century artistic reform, and they worked on many projects together. Although both were committed socialists, looking forward to an age of simple values and beliefs unfettered by capitalism, their own work was ironically beyond the means of most people.

Standen is the remaining intact example of Webb's mature work, and much of its interior, furniture and metalwork are his own designs. In the dining room seen here, the original blue-green paint of the panelling has faded a little with time and the dresser, designed by Webb, houses the type of blue and white porcelain of which Webb and Morris were particularly fond. Also on the dresser can be seen a teapot and stand and water jug, both by W A S Benson, together with an unusual muffin dish by C R Ashbee. The glass claret jug with silver mounts is by Christopher Dresser. The curtains are the original Peacock and Dragon design by William Morris in heavy wool tapestry. They are set against the same dark panelling framing Georgian-style windows overlooking a large sloping garden partly designed by G B Simpson, which stretches towards beautifully clear views of the Medway valley.

Original dark blue-green panelled walls by the architect Philip Webb are lightened by the softer green background of the William Morris tapestry curtains. A fine Liberty Guild oak table is surrounded by turn-of-the-century oak chairs with drop-in seats covered in the period design Ianthe

The dining table and chairs, from the Liberty Guild are still produced today. They are part of a collection of hand-crafted solid oak furniture inspired by the Arts and Crafts Movement and made in England. The fine oak table is a copy of a 1900 original by Liberty. On the table is a Tudric pewter bowl filled with fruit, supported by four cabriole legs with a stylized leaf decoration made by Liberty in 1902. A pair of Liberty Tudric pewter candlesticks, pierced central stems decorated with leaves and berries on tendrils were probably designed in 1905 by Archibald Knox, who worked closely with the store.

The oak chairs from the Liberty Guild Collection have drop-in seats which obviously had to be covered in fabric true to the period. Ianthe from the Chesham Collection, a popular pattern created in about 1900 by an unknown designer, was the ideal choice.

Main scheme fabric
Ianthe from the Chesham Collection
   Design no 1069604K, 135/138 cm (53/54 in) wide
   100% cotton, pattern repeat 31 cm (12¼ in)

The faded blues and maroons of Ianthe perfectly complement those of the carpet beneath and the glowing, mid-browns of the oak table, chair and wooden floorboards are enhanced by the brown tendrils of the print

——— ALTERNATIVE SCHEME ———
The best-selling peacock feather print Hera, from the Cotton Collection, is the natural alternative choice for the seat coverings. The design is by Arthur Silver, who was the founder of the Silver Studio and an important designer of Liberty textiles, silver and pewter, and dates from 1887. Its dark green background perfectly matches the painted wall panelling, the lighter green of the feathers emphasizing the soft green background of the William Morris curtains.

Alternative scheme fabric
Hera from the Cotton Collection
   Design no 1069635A, 135/138 cm (53/54 in) wide
   100% cotton, pattern repeat 36 cm (14¼ in)

Instructions
Drop-in chair seat cover with double piping and box edged sides (*see page 137*)

Ianthe

Hera

CONSERVATORY CHIC

Stone Green Hall is a hotel set in a little village in the Kent weald near Ashford. The present owners, who have lived at the Hall for seven years, have totally transformed a huge chilly looking conservatory into a sub-tropical garden for summer drinks and dining.

James and Ingrid Kempston bought the hall at Mersham although they originally intended to buy a house in East Anglia. But when they found Stone Green Hall (the main part of which is Queen Anne, built around a seventeenth century Cromwellian farmhouse) their plans rapidly changed.

Neither Mr or Mrs Kempston had any training in hotel management, but a measure of their success is that they have never needed to advertise. The house is run as a private one and a guest could find himself in a bedroom whose walls are lined with Williamsburg fabric added early in the house's history, with 1820s silk damask, or in panelling.

The large conservatory shown here was built by a previous owner, the late Peter Wilson, then chairman of Sotheby's, who was an enthusiastic gardener. In this large airy L-shaped space a mixture of bentwood and wickerwork, antique oak, modern beech and white gloss-painted furniture has been pulled together by the use of one fabric from Liberty's East India Collection, Santana.

This marvellous chintz is adapted from a Japanese screen, one of a panel of six, dating from the seventeenth century Edo period, and has been used here for table-cloths bound in a toning rose-coloured glazed chintz, which has also been used for the napkins. The softly faded wood

A view of one end of the conservatory, showing piped chintz cushions with ties, tablecloth and napkins

The modern beech director's chair shows how covering plain canvas with the right print can transform a relatively ordinary piece of furniture into something special

and brick-tiled floor are enhanced by the stippled and burnished background of the print, whose sun-washed reds are matched by a magnificent rank of exotic camelia trees, planted thirty years ago by the previous owner, and by the stronger reds of the geraniums. The result is a spectacular example of one fabric effecting a total mood change, making the conservatory a wonderful place in which to relax.

Main scheme fabric

Santana from the East India Collection
Design no 1143008A, 135/138 cm (53/54 in) wide
100% cotton glazed chintz, pattern repeat 64 cm (25¼ in)
Plain cotton glazed chintz, design no 1150001F, width as above

—— ALTERNATIVE SCHEME ——

The stripe Capriccio, from the East India Collection, offers a more modern approach picking up the red and green tones of the plants.

Alternative scheme fabric

Capriccio from the East India Collection
Design no 1143004G, 135/138 cm (53/54 in) wide
100% cotton glazed chintz, vertical stripe, pattern repeat 32 cm (12½ in)
Plain cotton glazed chintz, design no 1150001H, width as above

Instructions

Round tablecloth with bound edge (*see page 123*)
Napkins (*see page 139*)
Fabric-covered director's chair (*see page 136*)

Santana

Capriccio

DRINKS IN THE GARDEN

The five acre gardens surrounding Stone Green Hall, a small hotel near Ashford in Kent, are based on similar grounds in Hidcote, Gloucester. They were developed within the last thirty-five years by a previous owner of the house and keen horticulturalist, Peter Wilson, who laid them out in the grand manner to complement the Queen Anne period of the building.

Superb yew hedges form thick high walls which enclose amongst others a rose garden, a herbaceous garden, and a pond with gazebo—wonderful private places for assignations. The yew hedges surrounding the grass tennis court are over four metres (twelve feet) high, and in one of the walled gardens the owner, James Kempston, tends an impressive array of the herbs required for the excellent hotel restaurant for which he does all the cooking. His wife Ingrid gathers masses of fresh flowers every day from the various gardens with which to decorate the guest rooms.

These living walls create mysterious and secret environments, each with a different character. Randomly laid bricks and stone flags provide connecting pathways. Other paths have been laid to grass, flanked on the one side by yew walls and on the other by old fashioned pink and white roses. The eye is led naturally to a small white latticed gazebo set at one end of one of the paths against a copse of mature trees and guarded by dumpling shaped yew bushes. In other areas the yews have been clipped to form grand buttresses.

A small corner of the garden can be seen here, set with simple garden furniture in natural beech against a backdrop of wisteria and ball shaped yew bushes. The original canvas of the deckchairs has been covered in the fresh and pretty print Hedgerow, a 1960s design from the Cotton Collection. The lounger cushion, covered in the same print, is backed with a matching green towelling (terrycloth).

Main scheme fabric
Hedgerow from the Chesham II Collection
  Design no 1066014B, 135/138 cm (53/54 in) wide
  100% cotton, pattern repeat 64 cm (25¼ in) half drop

Modern natural
beechwood deck chairs
and a lounger covered in
the Hedgerow design in a
private corner of the yew
walled gardens of a
seventeenth century
Queen Anne hall

────── ALTERNATIVE SCHEME ──────
A cooler, more sophisticated effect is
created by the use of Tambourine from
the Chesham Collection, an ikat design
dating from the 1970s in muted shades of
dark green, blue and brick to blend in
with the colours of the garden and
pathway.

Alternative scheme fabric
Tambourine from the Chesham Collection
   Design no 1064637D, 135/138 cm (53/54 in)
   wide
   100% cotton, pattern repeat 46 cm (18 in)

Instructions
Fabric-covered deckchair (*see page 136*)
Buttoned lounger cushion (*see page 121*)

Alternative scheme illustrated overleaf

Hedgerow

Alternative scheme for Drinks in the Garden

Tambourine

THE CHELSEA ARTS CLUB

The club in London was founded in 1891 by Sterling Lee, Frank Brangwyn, George Clausen, James McNeil Whistler and Wilson Steer. Its aim was to provide a private club in which its members, originally from the painting, sculpting or architectural disciplines, would be able to relax in pleasant and congenial surroundings.

*E*ight years ago, although its rules remained intact, the membership of the Club had become seriously depleted and its marvellous old building, set in large grounds in Old Church Street in the heart of Chelsea, was in a very sad state of repair. It was then that Dudley and Mirjana Winterbottom, who owned and ran the Cherwell Boathouse Restaurant in Oxford, were invited to take over the running of the Club with which they fell in love.

The main club room is an enormous space with a gallery to one side reached by a narrow, winding staircase. Deep creamy yellow walls are hung with large canvases lent in an experimental three monthly exhibition by Royal Academicians, while two huge billiard tables straddle the parquet flooring. New cur-

Dark green carpeting in the gallery overlooking the club room is picked out in the green velvet piping of the cushions, providing a calm corner in which to read or play the piano

tains with matching self-piped tiebacks were chosen in the muted tones of Zebak from the Chesham Collection, blending beautifully with the old rugs, green baize and creamy walls of the room. Huge bay windows overlooking a garden complete with resident tortoise and frequented by Orlando, the Club's large ginger cat, are flanked with window seats covered in box edged cushions. Dark green velvet-piped scatter cushions are found in the green carpeted gallery above, which provides a cosy and comfortable hideaway where members can read or play the piano.

The use of the print Zebak has proved very successful: it does not detract from the paintings, it blends beautifully with the rugs and older furniture because of its traditional shapes, and looks wonderful in the soft evening glow of the table lights. Transformed by the Winterbottoms, the club now has the ambience of a large and relaxed household in which everyone comfortably co-exists.

Main scheme fabric
Zebak from the Chesham Collection
Design no 1064645A, 135/138 cm (53/54 in) wide
100% cotton, pattern repeat 64 cm ($25\frac{1}{4}$ in)

———— ALTERNATIVE SCHEME ————
Burnham, a pattern from the 1890s to 1900s, origin unknown, is a magnificent large scale print of leaves, grapes and flower heads in shades of burgundy, brown, navy and soft turquoise on a peach coloured background. Printed on heavyweight Union, it makes a spectacular alternative in this large room.

Alternative scheme fabric
Burnham from the Union Collection
Design no 1095107A, 135/138 cm (53/54 in) wide
53% linen, 35% cotton, 12% nylon, pattern repeat 46 cm (18 in)

Instructions
Curtains with locked-in lining (*see page 97*) with cartridge pleat heading (*see page 96*)
Shaped interlined tieback (*see page 109*)
Rectangular box edged cushion with piping (*see page 119*)
Roman blind (*see page 109*)
Alternative scheme illustrated overleaf

A huge bay window curtained in Zebak, a print inspired by the folded edges of kelims piled high one on top of the other

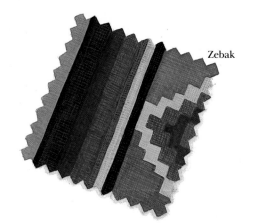
Zebak

Alternative scheme for Chelsea Arts Club

Burnham

ARTIST'S BEDROOM

The very pretty Sweet Pea print from an original drawing by the textile designer and flower artist Sidney Haward, who worked closely with Liberty around the turn of the century, is used here on a China blue background to decorate one of the thirteen guest bedrooms in the Chelsea Arts Club in London. Each bedroom is decorated differently and in this double bedded room overlooking beautiful gardens at the back of the building, curtains, blinds, tiebacks, and a covered curtain pole complete a coordinated look.

Paintings belonging to the Club and the work of members both past and present (club rules dictate that seventy per cent of its members must practise art of some form) are hung at every opportunity up the staircases and along the landings leading off to the bedrooms, one whole corridor being given over to the work of its photographer members. In the hall downstairs a monthly exhibition is held of members' work, each exhibition having a different theme, and all the work is for sale. In the large dining room overlooking the garden, which contains a fountain in the last stages of restoration, further canvases are hung; this room is filled by an enormous wooden dining table at which everyone sits for breakfast.

The Sweet Pea design in this bedroom was chosen to coordinate with the deeper blue carpet already in position, and to bring freshness to the room. The fitted and gusseted bed covers are piped in the darker blue of the carpet. The curtains have a cased heading and the pole is covered to match. The metal arms fixed to each side of the window to hold the curtains in place are covered with a matching fabric casing to complete the look. The window recess holds a ruffled Austrian blind which softens the window and detracts from its height. Members are delighted with the finished effect, which shows how easily a quite ordinary room can be transformed into a pretty and welcoming one, by the use of one well-chosen print.

Main scheme fabric

Sweet Pea from the Cotton Collection
   Design no 1061613D, 135/138 cm (53/54 in) wide
   100% cotton, pattern repeat 64 cm (25¼ in)

Sweet Pea print is used to cover pole, pole ends and to provide cased, fixed curtains. It prettifies an essentially plain bedroom and provides softened, diffused light through unlined Austrian blinds set in a recessed window

A ruffled Austrian blind set in the window recess directs the light downwards to give a gentle diffused glow

—— ALTERNATIVE SCHEME ——
Willow from the Cotton Collection, a flowing design of pale blue and white adapted from a William Morris print, is a pretty alternative to Sweet Pea. The blue of the print tones with the carpet and provides softness in a white-walled room.

Alternative scheme fabric
Willow from the Cotton Collection
    Design no 1069620L, 135/138 cm (53/54 in) wide
    100% cotton, pattern repeat 32 cm (12½ in)

Instructions
Fixed curtains (*see page 99*)
Ruffled casing for metal arm (*see page 106*)
Unlined Austrian blind with double ruffle (*see page 111*)
Fitted and piped bedspread with pillow gussets and kick pleats (*see page 125*)
Pole cover (*see page 139*)

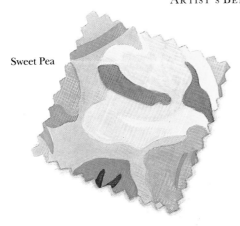

Sweet Pea

Willow

ESSENCE OF THE ORIENT

A Coromandel incised lacquer screen of the late seventeenth century is the inspiration behind the marvellously designed chintz fabric and wallpaper set in the living room of its designer, David Haward, in a large and spacious house in Strawberry Hill on the outskirts of London.

A consultant designer for Liberty of London Prints Ltd and great-nephew of Sidney Haward, David runs an independent fabric design studio from his home, a business which also services other large furnishing fabric companies. His creative sources are varied. David Haward's collection of old Poole pottery formed the basis of a design story sold in the States and many of his designs, taken from seventeenth and eighteenth century Eastern screens, are in the East India Collection of fabrics.

Choosing one of his own designs for his

The elegant china blue print of Suki chintz with its matching wallpaper and border, is shown in luxurious relief in swags and lined tails (jabots) draped in sculpted folds across a bay window

Cartridge pleat curtains in Suki chintz from the East India Collection are lined and interlined to give a rich warm feel to the lounge. Small tails (jabots) punctuate the lush swags between them and the matching wallpaper and border pick out the soft faded pink of both prints, further emphasized by the Moorcroft ceramic pieces beneath

living room, the designer went for the smokey blue-grey chintz of Suki from the East India Collection which one might have thought would look cold. On the contrary, it provides an oasis of peace, warmth and elegance which tones beautifully with the deep blue-grey of the ceiling. Two Moorcroft pieces can be seen on the small side table. Paintings by Allingham, a turn-of-the-century artist whose work was found in David's father's attic during a move, every canvas incidentally having been used as a palette on its wrong side, are now restored and hung, depicting scenes from a small area of Normandy. The Persian is one of an extended family of six cats that share the house, having full rein in the studio. An old sofa not in the picture is the designer's only bugbear. It remains undecorated until exactly the right fabric is found for it, but of course, once finished, the room will no longer be a challenge or give the excitement it now does, as there will be nothing left to improve or create anew.

Main scheme fabric
Suki from the East India Collection
    Design no 1143001E, 135/138 cm (53/54 in) wide
    100% cotton glazed chintz, pattern repeat 64 cm (25¼ in)

—— ALTERNATIVE SCHEME ——
Melbury from the Chesham II Collection, the original design of which is in the Victoria and Albert Museum, Kensington, provides a total contrast in soft faded shades of fawn, brown and china blue against walls painted a plain cream.

Alternative scheme fabric
Melbury from the Chesham II Collection
    Design no 1066009E, 135/138 cm (53/54 in) wide
    100% cotton, pattern repeat 51 cm (20 in)

Instructions
Swags and tails (jabots) for a bay window
    (*see page 102*)
Interlined curtains with handmade triple cartridge pleat heading (*see page 98*)
Shaped interlined tieback (*see page 109*)

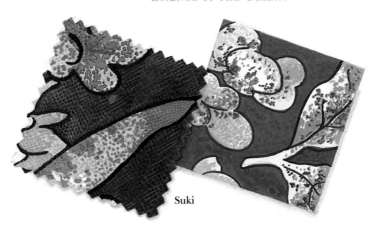

Suki

Melbury

COUNTRY PATCHWORK

A Tana lawn patchwork bedspread in random log cabin design makes an ideal bedcovering in a late sixteenth century red brick country farmhouse set amongst four hundred acres of Kent farmland. Flower printed curtains carry through the country theme.

The bedroom came as a complete surprise to the wife of the owner, as he organized its redecoration in her absence. The pinch pleat curtains are made up in the design Petronella from the Chesham II Collection and the peach, pink and beige shades tone with the wood panelling and the bedspread. The patchwork is made up to gentle effect in a selection of Tana lawns.

Tana lawn was introduced to Liberty in the 1920s by a former cotton buyer and later director of Liberty, William Haynes Dorrell. An enormous amount of preparation goes into the weaving and finishing of this fine quality cloth made from Egyptian and Peruvian yarn, which is printed predominantly in England, each design being carefully colour matched to provide a colour story within the context of a whole range.

To complete the decoration of the room, a Victorian firescreen of berries and autumn leaves is set in an old brick fireplace above which is hung one of a number of Victorian watercolours of country scenes collected by the owners.

Main scheme fabric
Petronella from the Chesham II Collection
  Design no 1066007C, 135/138 cm (53/54 in) wide
  100% cotton, pattern repeat 46 cm (18 in) half drop

A Tana lawn patchwork bedspread in log cabin design forms the central focus of this sixteenth century farmhouse bedroom, decorated in shades of pale peach to complement the Petronella floral design of the pinch pleat curtains

The soft peach and pink curtain shades of an original design from the turn of the century by flower artist and textile designer Sidney Haward, who worked closely with Liberty, are picked out in the panelling

—— ALTERNATIVE SCHEME ——
Hermia, a print of faded brown roses and pale grey wisteria set against muted shades of grey and blue-green foliage and pale oak lattice work, blends unobtrusively with the bedspread and harmonizes with the soft tones of the bedroom.

Alternative scheme fabric
Hermia from the Chesham II Collection
    Design no 1066005A, 135/138 cm (53/54 in)
    wide
    100% cotton, pattern repeat 64 cm (25¼ in)

Instructions
Patchwork bedspread (*may be bought at Liberty*) (*see page 128*)
Square patchwork (make as above) cushions (*may be bought at Liberty*) (*see page 128*)
Curtains with locked-in lining (*see page 97*) with pinch pleat heading (*see page 96*)

Petronella

Hermia

Teenage Studio

The prime need of a seventeen-year-old girl must be for a place of her own. In the large and airy room featured here, parental inspiration is behind a well organized decorative theme, which has been created with a minimum of fuss and expense.

Beige carpeting, cream walls and white gloss wood-work provide an ideal backdrop for colour. With the addition of a lined throwover bedspread and large piped floor cushion together with a few smaller scatter cushions in the strong print Zebak from the Chesham Collection, in a colourway that ties up with the reds and blues of the prints and divan surround and the existing blue floor cushion, the whole is lifted and pulled together for minimal expenditure.

The print design Zebak is a new one, launched in 1984. It was developed by John Laflin, Design Director of Liberty of London Prints Ltd. On walking through the oriental carpet department on the third floor of the Liberty store in Regent Street, London, he noticed how beautiful the edges of the stacked kelims looked in combination. Their colour tones and varied designs blended so well that he took some colour photos of the stacked rugs, with the result that Zebak was born, a ten-colour print of immense character that lends itself as easily to a modern studio as to an old wood panelled room.

In this room the intention was to create a strong, cleanly modern look by using very simple, easily-made furnishings which could be changed at will to create another totally different feel to the same backdrop, and which would also be ideal for rented accommodation.

The narrow stripes of
modern aluminium
blinds echo the wider
stripes of the Zebak
printed floor cushion

A simple lined
bedspread with
matching scatter
cushions in the kelim-
inspired print Zebak,
creates instant design
impact in a teenager's
studio

Main scheme fabric
Zebak from the Chesham Collection
  Design no 1064645A, 135/138 cm (53/54 in)
  wide
  100% cotton, pattern repeat 64 cm ($25\frac{1}{4}$ in)

Alternative scheme fabric
Scherzo from the Chesham II Collection
  Design no 1066001C, 135/138 cm (53/54 in)
  wide
  100% cotton, pattern repeat 64 cm ($25\frac{1}{4}$ in)
  half drop

———— ALTERNATIVE SCHEME ————
The print Scherzo, from the Chesham II
Collection, a tongue-in-cheek paisley
design, provides a lively modern feel to
the room while blending in with the reds
and blues of the prints and divan
surround.

Instructions
Square cushion (*see page 117*) **with piping**
  (*see page 141*)
Lined bedspread (*see page 125*)

Zebak

Scherzo

ASCOT BOX

The walls of most boxes at this world-renowned racecourse in the Berkshire country-side are hung with the obligatory racing prints, but in this box, seating ten people, a quite different and totally refreshing effect has been achieved by the imaginative use of three fabrics.

The oriental pavilion featured here belongs to Liberal MP Clement Freud, the writer, broadcaster and culinary expert, who is also a racing enthusiast. His choice of brilliant lacquer reds in such an enclosed space may at first seem startling, but the overall result is quite spectacular. He loved the bright, racy red of the oriental print Bladon from the East India Collection, adapted from a late nineteenth century design showing the influence of both Indian calico print and Chinoiserie design, which he felt would counteract the dungeon-like qualities of the box. One wall was lined with mirrored glass in order to give the illusion of space and Bladon was used to make pinch pleat curtains, which are lined in a strong green matching the leaf colouring in the print.

Contrast-piped and shaped tiebacks sporting neat rosettes hold the curtaining in place, while the dark understair alcove is made cosy by a fabric covered wall, richly gathered and slung between three poles, in the Tana lawn print Mayfair. This paisley print is used again for the contrast-piped cushions set behind a black sofa, lightened by further cushions in Bladon and its coordinating stripe Capriccio, also from the East India Collection.

Crowning the box hangs a lush tented ceiling that uses over 33 metres (36 yards) of fabric. The use of the Capriccio stripe lifts the eye upwards, giving an illusion of height. The 'central' point of

A flamboyant oriental pavilion, the perfect setting for watching the Ascot races

A warm and cosy corner
is created by covering an
alcove wall in lavishly
gathered paisley print
Mayfair from the Tana
Lawn Collection,
matched by plump piped
cushions

the ceiling, the gathered choux, is butted up to the mirror which reflects the half ceiling to create a full square. Covered fillets in the Bladon print neatly finish the tent edges.

Natural beech furniture and beige carpet form a calm focal point for the eye and the whole exudes a flamboyant and happy feeling of exotic warmth and comfort which makes the business of the race more exciting, the day a more special outing.

Fabric
Bladon from the East India Collection
    Design no 1143003C, 135/138 cm (53/54 in) wide
    100% cotton glazed chintz, pattern repeat 64 cm (25¼ in) half drop

Capriccio from the East India Collection
    Design no 1143004F, 135/138 cm (53/54 in) wide
    100% cotton glazed chintz, vertical stripe, pattern repeat 32 cm (12½ in)

Mayfair from the Tana Lawn Collection
    Design no 3336040B, 90 cm (35 in) wide
    100% cotton lawn

Instructions
Gathered tented ceiling (*see page 132*)
Curtains with locked-in lining (*see page 97*)
    with triple pinch pleat heading (*see page 96*)
Gathered fabric wall (*see page 133*)
Square cushion cover (*see page 117*) with
    piping (*see page 141*)

ALGONQUIN SUITE

The Algonquin Hotel at 59 West 44th Street in New York, long a favourite for its literary history and friendly atmosphere, contains two suites decorated in Liberty fabrics which were originally refurbished at the time of the Festival of Britain in the United States, and entitled 'Festival' suites.

The Algonquin rise to fame as a literary watering-hole began in about 1914 with the patronage of the iconoclast, lexicographer and newspaperman H L Mencken. It was frequented by such luminaries as William Faulkner, James Thurber, Gertrude Stein, Graham Greene, Tennessee Williams and F Scott Fitzgerald. In 1919, Robert Benchley and Dorothy Parker took part in the meetings of the Round Table club. This 'inner circle' progressed through the Thanatopsis Poker and Literary Club to become the Thanatopsis Poker and Inside Straight Club, and it was as a result of these meetings at the hotel that Harold Ross created the *New Yorker* magazine to encapsulate the humorous outpourings of his friends.

Quilted and piped bedspreads are matched by cased curtains, which are bound in the green of the carpet, providing a link between sitting room and bedroom in this American interpretation of British style

The Algonquin's rooms have now been restored to their original casual sophistication, and its lobby, lounge and restaurant are still a favourite and fashionable haunt of many literary and theatrical personalities. During a celebration of all things British, Liberty fabrics were used in the redecoration of the two 'Festival' suites, in an American interpretation of comfortable 'English country home' style.

The walls of the sitting room pictured here have been decorated in British racing green eggshell paint in a shade darker than that of the carpet, and this background colouring provides a warm and comfortable setting for the stylish Petronella from the Chesham II Collection, a design of peonies in frilly full bloom. Its peach shades are offset by dark green foliage, and curtains have been lined and bound to match.

Similar treatment has been given to the quilted bedspreads, which are lightened by the use of paler green valances (dust ruffles), while a very pretty, classic armchair has been covered in the totally contrasting print Terrace from the Cotton Collection, a simple geometric design. Ruffled cushions and the chair with its drop-in seat in Tana lawn were bought rather than made and introduce a third print reflecting the peach of the large-flowered Petronella.

Fabric

Petronella from the Chesham II Collection
   Design no 1066007C, 135/138 cm (53/54 in) wide
   100% cotton, pattern repeat 46 cm (18 in) half drop

Terrace from the Cotton Collection
   Design no 1069657G, 135/138 cm (53/54 in) wide
   100% cotton, pattern repeat 6 cm ($2\frac{1}{2}$ in)

Instructions

SITTING ROOM:
Curtains with locked-in lining (*see page 97*) with cartridge pleat heading (*see page 96*)
Piped pelmet (cornice) with lined contrast edge ruffle (*see page 106*)
BEDROOM:
Fitted quilted bedspread with contrast piping (*see page 130*)
Ruffled valance (dust ruffle) (*see page 129*)
Curtains with sewn-in lining and contrast piping on inner edges (*see page 97*)

The turn-of-the-century
print Petronella provides
a pretty and
sophisticated focus in
one of the 'Festival'
suites at the Algonquin
Hotel, New York

COTTAGE SEWING ROOM

The village of Westerham in Kent is set among open farmland near Chartwell, home of the late Sir Winston Churchill. It is also the setting for several Tudor cottages built around 1540 during the last few years of the reign of Henry VIII.

At the turn of the century three of these cottages were converted into one larger, L-shaped house, now owned by the cookery writer Susanna Tee and her husband. It is a listed building and the house still retains its original timber framing and low beams. The house boasts several inglenook fireplaces, a bread oven, four attic rooms each of which is reached by a separate staircase from the first floor, small leaded light windows and a wealth of character.

Susanna's sewing room, in what would have been a bedroom in the original cottage, is a private wood-beamed room in which she can tuck herself away. At the end of a sewing session she can leave the sewing machine in position ready for the next bout and close the door on the piles of fabric, half-finished dresses and trails of threads which are the hallmark of a home dressmaker. She thinks of this room as a luxury and, being an avid collector of Liberty fabric, fell in love with the Clandon print from the Chesham II Collection which she felt matched the cottagey feel of the room.

The use of smocked tape as a heading for the curtains and as a means of gathering the stool cover works well in the

Smock-headed curtains in Clandon print, a mass of Spring flowers, provide the perfect match for the sewing room of a 1540s timber-framed Tudor cottage

context of this rustic room, as do the wooden rings and pole which enhance the period and the feel of the room. The deep blue colouring of a mass of narcissi, daffodils, freesia and tulips shot through with dusky pink, red and wine complement the dark beams and leaded windows perfectly.

Fabric
Clandon from the Chesham II Collection
 Design no 1066008E, 135/138 cm (53/54 in) wide
 100% cotton, pattern repeat 31 cm (12$\frac{1}{4}$ in) half drop

Instructions
Curtains with locked-in lining (*see page 97*)
 with smocked heading (*see page 94*)
Smocked stool cover (*see page 137*)
Smocked tieback (*see page 107*)

CONTEMPORARY KITCHEN

A terraced cottage in London is the setting for this spacious kitchen-cum-dining room where the choice of the vinyl coated print Bauhaus from the Chesham Collection in vivid shades of green, blue, red, pink, maroon and yellow provides a strong focal point to the room.

The wooden cupboards of the kitchen have been transformed by dark green lacquer coach paint and bright red handles into a stylish range of units. The clever use of original green enamelled 1920s schoolhouse lightshades gives a period feel to the room and the primary colours of the tablecloth and chair cushions work particularly well in a kitchen that has to be both a functional and pleasant sit-down area.

The Bauhaus print is adapted from an original tapestry designed by Gunta Stölzl, of the Bauhaus school, in 1926/27. Although commonly assumed to be a design movement of the 1920s and 1930s, Bauhaus was in fact an art school founded in Dessau, East Germany by the architect Walter Gropius and employing as staff some of the foremost painters, architects and designers of the time. This school was seen as the essence of the Modern Movement, yet it adopted many of the ideals of the Arts and Crafts Movement, such as simplicity of design, but unlike the practitioners of Arts and Crafts the Bauhaus did not disdain machines. The approach to design was to stress aesthetic fundamentals and to strive for geometrically pure forms. Since the school's closure in 1933, Bauhaus has become synonymous with the machine age in art and design, and its influence is felt here in this print.

A Bauhaus print, taken from an original tapestry of the Twenties by Gunta Stölzl is used here in vinyl coated form for a round tablecloth and knife-edged chair cushions

Fabric
Bauhaus from the Chesham Collection
  Design no 1069663B, 135/138 cm (53/54 in) wide
  100% cotton, PVC coated to order, pattern repeat 64 cm (25¼ in) half drop

Instructions
Round vinyl coated tablecloth (*see page 123*)
Square cushion cover (*see page 117*)

OAK PANELLED OFFICE

Rich dark oak panelling lines the walls of an old farm office from which a four hundred acre farm is managed. This panelling dates from the building of the farmhouse in 1637 and provides a wonderfully warm and cosy environment in which to work.

The print chosen for the pinch pleat curtains at the window and for the ruffled pelmet (cornice) is Melrose from the Chesham Collection. Its sophisticated yet homely design of vines, grapes, tropical fruit and exotic birds sporting important tail feathers, together with an occasional brightly coloured butterfly, furnishes a celebration of colour in this tiny room.

The curtains have been lined in the lighter, soft rose colouring of the tropical fruit, whilst the deeper maroon-brown of the grapes, which so richly complements the woodwork, is matched by silky tasselled cord tiebacks for a period touch. A simple terracotta pot of red geraniums picks out the scarlet colouring of the riper fruit, also reflected in the bright red neck feathers of the birds and the contrast piping on the pelmet (cornice). A well filled, box edged cushion with contrast piping is attached by ties of scarlet to the struts of a comfortable office chair.

Furnishing the office, an inlaid mother-of-pearl Victorian letter rack holds urgent post, files are set in matter-of-fact manner to one side of the recess, and a large metal spike holds paid bills firmly in position. A standard 1929 General Post Office desk telephone, a British design

discontinued in 1936, is set at one side of the desk top. A small Edwardian glass shade gives unobtrusive light from above, while the brass handles of the desk are reflected in a brass desk lamp. High on a corner shelf, old leather bound volumes are a reminder of the age and history of the farm. The overall feeling of this small room is one of durability and practicality.

Fabric
Melrose from the Chesham Collection
  Design no 1069679A, 135/138 cm (53/54 in) wide
  100% cotton, pattern repeat 36 cm (14¼ in)

Instructions
Curtains with locked-in lining (*see page 97*)
  with pinch pleat heading (*see page 96*)
Pelmet (cornice) with piping and double ruffle (*see page 105*)
Round box edged cushion (*see page 120*) **with contrast piping** (*see page 141*)

The rich and glowing print Melrose, a celebration of vines, tropical fruit and birds, is employed here to complement seventeenth century oak panelling in the small office of a Kent farmhouse

A BOY'S BEDROOM

The decoration of a nine-year-old boy's bedroom which will stand the test of the years into his teens may seem an impossible goal to achieve. However, for Charlie, living with his family in London, a happy solution has been found which pleases him and his mother equally.

Charlie is a boisterous youngster who, when his turn came to choose fabric for the redecoration of his room, voiced a strong preference for red. His mother, however, realizing that he would quickly tire of a very bright colour, encouraged him towards the more muted shades of Bauhaus and Kasak, whose detailed designs would disguise the effects of dirty fingers. These he was very pleased with; they toned well with his soft beige carpet and fitted in nicely with the dark wood colouring of his desk and chair.

A Roman blind was made up in Bauhaus from the Chesham Collection in shades of grey, air force blue, muted navy, dulled rusts and peaches, the abstract design and masculine colouring of which he approved. Bauhaus is complemented by the design Kasak, also from the Chesham Collection, a design by Susan Collier inspired by the work of Sonia Delaunay, who was a pioneer of abstract painting from the early part of this century.

The floor cushion made up on one side in the print Kasak and on the other, Bauhaus in the same shades provides useful additional seating for Charlie, who spends much of his spare time developing the tracking of his train set. These prints will also take a fair amount

of hard wear before beginning to look grubby. Since this picture was taken, Charlie's padded headboard has been recovered in the same Bauhaus print. His mother has also made up a throwover bedspread in Bauhaus, with which she is delighted, and the colours of the print together with the carpet and contrasting cushion result in a happy and practical solution for a growing boy's bedroom.

Fabric
Bauhaus from the Chesham Collection
   Design no 1069663F, 135/138 cm (53/54 in) wide
   100% cotton, pattern repeat 64 cm ($25\frac{1}{4}$ in) half drop

Kasak from the Chesham Collection
   Design no 1069624F, 135/138 cm (53/54 in) wide
   100% cotton, pattern repeat 41 cm ($16\frac{1}{4}$ in)

Instructions
Roman blind (*see page 109*)
Square cushion cover (*see page 117*) with
   piping (*see page 142*)

**A geometric design suits
the neat tailored lines of
a Roman blind**

MARBLED BATHROOM

Pale grey Carrara marble from the hills of North West Italy has been used throughout this bathroom to line the walls and floor and gives a modern clean impression to the room.

Against this quiet backdrop hangs a Liberty print roller blind in the design Kasak from the Chesham Collection. This was introduced in the early 1970s and has been used here in shades of pale and darker greys, fawn, taupe, muted grey-green and brown interspersed by the occasional splash of black against a background of pinky beige. It is a painterly design which works perfectly in very modern surroundings, giving a warm glow to this small room. The grey marbling in this bathroom encourages a feeling of spaciousness and is, of course, immensely practical to maintain.

In the rest of this London home, grey-stained floors and white walls throughout provide an exciting and serious backdrop for the owner's collection of contemporary paintings and for important pieces of furniture. The use of white, grey and other neutrals in the house creates a feeling of continuity and peace which extends into the bathroom.

Fabric
Kasak from the Chesham Collection
Design no 1069624F, 135/138 cm (53/54 in) wide
100% cotton, pattern repeat 41 cm (16¼ in)

Instructions
Roller blind (*see page 112*)

Kasak is used in shades
of grey, fawn, muted
green and brown to
warm the pale grey tones
of Carrara marble in this
modern bathroom

BABY BLUES

A Moses basket (bassinet) is an ideal light-weight carrycot for a small baby, and the basket shown here is particularly prettily decked out. One of the very soft Tana lawn prints has been used to make its lining and coverlet, and the lining for the basket that holds the baby's essentials.

Tana lawn has been printed by Liberty since the 1920s, when it was made of long staple cotton, grown near Lake Tana in Ethiopia, hence its name. Many of the beautiful little floral, geometric and paisley prints were taken from old block impressions in books. Other prints originated from bunches of flowers picked from around the studio in Merton Abbey, but nowadays screens have surplanted the blocks, some of which are in the Victoria and Albert Museum and others in private collections.

The sides of the Moses basket (bassinet) have been lined with one particularly pretty print which has been quilted to make it beautifully soft and cosy. This quilting is attached to an unquilted base, on top of which sits a fitted baby mattress with a washable cover. A deep ruffle has been added to the top of the quilting, split open at each side to allow the handles of the basket to protrude and coordinating ribbons tie the opening at the handles together.

Broderie anglaise (eyelet edging) is the ideal finishing touch for the ruffle edging, a detail which extends to the quilted coverlet. A smaller basket has been lined in matching quilted lawn, with a gathered broderie anglaise (eyelet edging) ruffle around its rim. Two blue

and white teddies, one older and more loved than the other, complete this charming picture.

Fabric
Classic Tana lawn
  Design no 3336031B, 90 cm (35 in) wide
  100% cotton lawn
  It should be borne in mind that Tana lawn is *not* suitable for furnishing but appeals to those who like the typical Liberty floral look.

Instructions
Quilted Moses basket (bassinet) with matching coverlet (*see page 134*)
Basket with quilted lining (*see page 136*)

A lined, ruffled and quilted Moses basket (bassinet) with matching coverlet provides a safe, comfy and pretty environment for a small baby

THEATRICAL BACKDROP

Dramatic curtaining frames one of the tall windows of an Eaton Terrace home acquired by its owner some three years ago, and now undergoing stage-by-stage refurbishment. The houses of this area of central London were built between 1830 and 1840 and possess lofty, spacious rooms which give plenty of scope for decoration.

Since the owner of this house is an avid collector of tapestries, rugs and antique wall hangings, he has a strong preference for white walls and neutral carpets which form a plain backdrop. Anatolian kelims from the mountainous Asian region of Turkey feature strongly in the collection, as do Chinese opera robes and Thai wall hangings. It was felt that the richness of this collection would be best enhanced by the use of a richly coloured, plain fabric.

The plain gunmetal grey glazed chintz decided on for the cartridge pleat curtains are lined and interlined to make them drape well. The curtains drape on to the carpet for dramatic effect and are held in place with tasselled cord tiebacks. Swag and tails (jabots) are lined in contrasting bois-de-rose glazed cotton.

Fabric
Design no 1150001A (gunmetal grey) and 1150001N (bois-de-rose), 135/138 cm (53/54 in) wide
100% cotton glazed chintz

Instructions
Interlined curtains with triple pinch pleat heading *(see page 98)*
Swag and contrast-lined tails (jabots) *(see page 104)*

Heavy cartridge pleat glazed cotton curtains with matching bois-de-rose lined swag and tails (jabots) look timelessly elegant and blend with an eclectic collection of kelims, wall hangings and Chinese opera robes

EASTERN PROMISE

A spectacular quilted and lined bedspread featuring Chinese dragons, clouds and border print, makes a stunning addition to a lovely antique bedstead found discarded at the back of a country antique store.

The designer, whose bedroom this is, was originally inspired by a similar quilt made for the launch in March 1984 of the Liberty chintz range of furnishing fabrics entitled the East India Collection. He found the quilt 'totally over the top', had to have it, and was reduced to ordering the fabric and having a similar one made.

This type of one-off design will certainly become one of the antiques of the future. The bedspread is made from Opium, a fabric design adapted from a Coromandel incised lacquer screen of the late seventeenth century, and reversed with Suki, a design of oriental flowers in bowls from the same source and period. It makes stunning use of the borders of the Opium print, which are cut out to make four long panels of dragons with surrounding clouds. The border sections of the fabric are set at each side of the quilt and form dividing lines between each panel. A smaller strip using up the remaining border print is set at top and bottom of the covering. The panels are backed with wadding (batting) and each of the dragons, their flames, legs, claws and clouds are stitched round, giving them a three-dimensional effect. The panels are joined down the length to make a complete bedspread. Left-over areas of the central print designs of both Suki and Opium are made use of in

scatter cushions in square, round and heart shapes, which are piled high on the bed, while the soft deep blue of the ceiling creates an exotic oriental night sky.

The origin of the Chinese lacquer screen from which these designs come takes its name from the Coromandel Coast along the Bay of Bengal in South East India, where a great deal of trading both by the East India Company and by others from Holland, France and Denmark, took place throughout the seventeenth, eighteenth and nineteenth centuries. A modern Japanese six-panelled and mother-of-pearl inlaid screen, one of a selection at Liberty, beautifully emphasizes the oriental ambience of the room, while a Tiffany-style lamp, also from Liberty, gives a warm feeling to the bedroom.

Fabric

Opium from the East India Collection
  Design no 1143002A, 135/138 cm (53/54 in) wide
  100% cotton glazed chintz, pattern repeat 64 cm (25¼ in)

Suki from the East India Collection
  Design no 1143001A, 135/138 cm (53/54 in) wide
  100% cotton glazed chintz, pattern repeat 64 cm (25¼ in)

Instructions

Lined bedspread with quilted dragon panels
  (*see page 131*)
Square cushion cover (*see page 117*) with piping (*see page 142*)
Square cushion cover (*see page 117*) with double ruffle (*see page 142*)
Heart-shaped cushion cover with double ruffle and piping (*see page 119*)

A spectacular quilted bedspread with Chinese dragons, clouds and strong border design is piled high with matching ruffled and piped scatter cushions to provide a rich oriental covering for an antique wooden bedstead

An Attic Window

Many attic bedrooms now have modern windows inserted in the pitched roof to provide extra light. Because of the simplicity of this spare bedroom, recently decorated in pale shades of blue and white to emphasize the lightness of the room, the owners of this London house wanted a fresh and pretty print for the roller blind that was to be set at the window.

A basic roller blind kit and three wooden slats were purchased. One of these slats was inserted through a casing at the base of the roller blind. As the slat protrudes at either side it could be slotted into grooves cut in the remaining slats that were cut and fixed at each side of the window, giving different positions of closure. The lower edge of each side slat was rounded off so that the bottom of the blind would slot easily into position and then painted to match the surrounding frame.

The blind was made up in the usual way, tensioning it higher than normal to prevent it sagging at this unusual angle. The cool blue colourway of the Willow print from the Cotton Collection was used for the blind, a lovely flowing print of willow leaves adapted from a design by William Morris which fits in well with the modern surround of the window. Light filtering into the room through so pale a print gives a soft diffused glow.

Houses on the Peterborough Estate in Fulham, where this one is situated, were built in the 1890s for skilled artisans and their families and sport stone lions on the parapets of their roofs. A guest in this house, therefore, pulling open the blind in the morning, is treated to a little of London's history at a closer angle than would otherwise have been possible.

Fabric
Willow from the Cotton Collection
 Design no 1069620L, 135/138 cm (53/54 in) wide
 100% cotton, pattern repeat 32 cm (12½ in)

Instructions
Roller blind (*see page 112*)

Willow design from the
Cotton Collection is the
very pretty flowing print
used here in the simple
but successful treatment
of a slanting attic
bedroom window

If a track is going to show, choose one that is unobtrusive or a decorative one that blends in with the curtaining. Some tracks can be painted or covered with fabric. Poles are meant to be displayed, the curtains hanging below from wooden or brass rings.

There are many types of track and pole to choose from. Large department stores often have displays of curtain hardware where you can compare prices and functions. Flexible tracks will bend easily if you are making curtains to fit round a curved window; wooden poles can be mitred to fit round bays. Tracks are usually sold with runners. Most poles are packed complete with rings, brackets, screws and finials, and some are extendible. If you are making heavy curtains, buy a track or pole with an integral cording set to making drawing easy. Some manufacturers also offer curtain and valance tracks combined in one fitting.

Hooks for use in drawstring heading tape are made in metal or plastic, have a double bend and are threaded through the slots in the tape. Those used for hand-pleated headings are pronged and are pushed into the slots along the back of the tape to make groups of pleats. Hooks used for handmade headings are either the steel pin variety that are stabbed into the back of the heading to secure them or they are sewn on by hand. Both pin and pronged hooks come with long and short necks so the curtain can hang below a pole or the heading extend above a track. Match the hook to the track or pole used and allow one hook and runner to every 8 cm ($3\frac{1}{4}$ in) of curtain, plus one for each end.

Lead weights can be inserted in the hems of curtains to make them hang better. These are stitched into the mitre at each corner. Weighted tape can also be bought by the metre (yard) and laid along the base of the curtain hem.

LININGS, INTERLININGS AND STIFFENINGS

Linings ensure that curtains drape well, giving them body and fullness; they protect the fabric from light, noise and dirt and help insulate the room.

Most linings are made from 100 per cent cotton sateen and are available in a range of colours, besides the usual beige, which is also generally the cheapest. Choose the best lining you can afford because a poor one will wear out long before the curtains. Lining sateen is very closely and unevenly woven, so do not try to tear it when preparing lengths.

Detachable linings can be used for lightweight or open-weave curtains. They do not drape as well, but are easily removed for washing and can be detached during warmer months. They are made up in the same way as an unlined curtain (see page 96). Special heading tape for detachable linings enables you to hang the lining on the same hook as the curtain.

An interlining is the extra layer that can be stitched between the curtain fabric and the lining. Besides giving the curtain a plump luxurious look, it cuts out light and provides insulation. Soft and loosely woven, it comes in several thicknesses. In the UK bump is the thickest, and looks like a fleecy blanket; domette is a finer fluffy fabric suitable for interlining less heavy curtains. Both are cotton. In the USA flannel and flannelette are usually used. Both are lighter than bump and domette. There are also synthetic interlinings, which drape well and don't produce fluff or stretch when handled, but they do not block out light as effectively.

When hand-making headings for curtains you will need to use a buckram stiffening. This can be purchased in depths of 10 cm (4 in), 12 cm (5 in) or 15 cm (6 in) and it is attached to the back of the curtain top.

MEASURING FOR CURTAINS

Always measure for curtains with the track or pole in position (cased curtains are dealt with separately on page 99). These can be mounted within the window recess or extend either side of the window frame so that there is enough room for the curtains to be pulled back from the window. The height of the track above the window will

Fig 1   Overlap allowance

Sill length

Floor length

depend on the visual effect you want your curtains to make. Between 7.5 cm (3 in) and 12 cm (5 in) above the window is usual (fig 1).

1 Measure the length of the track or pole. Multiply this figure by the heading fullness required (see page 94). To this amount add 5 cm (2 in) for each side hem. Add an allowance for the overlap if you have a track with an overlap arm.

2 Divide this total by one fabric width (usually 122 cm/48 in or 137 cm/54 in), rounding up this calculation to the nearest width. (Unless you are making curtains for a very narrow window you will have to join widths to make up each curtain and you should therefore allow an extra 1.5 cm/$\frac{5}{8}$ in for each seam allowance.)

3 For divided curtains halve this amount to get the number of widths needed per curtain. Position any half widths at outer edges of each curtain.

4 Next measure off the desired length of the curtain from the rings on the track runners or from just under the pole.

5 Add the top hem/heading allowance. Allow a 3 cm ($1\frac{1}{4}$ in) top hem for a handmade or ready-made heading if you are hanging the curtain from a pole. To cover a track, curtains should hang from the middle or lower row of slots on ready-made heading tape. Measure from the top of these slots (the point at which the curtains are suspended) to the top of the tape and add this

distance plus 3 cm ($1\frac{1}{4}$ in) to the length measurement (fig 1). Allow sufficient heading above the suspension point on a hand-pleated or handmade heading to cover the track. Add this measurement plus 3 cm ($1\frac{1}{4}$ in) top hem to the length.

6 Add a 10 cm (4 in) base hem allowance to the overall length. Then deduct 1 cm ($\frac{3}{8}$ in) for floor- and sill-length curtains. Add at least an extra 7.5 cm (3 in) for curtains to drape on to the floor.

7 Multiply the length by the number of widths needed for the curtains to get the total amount of fabric.

8 Patterned fabric should be matched across seams and at the centre of a pair of curtains when closed. This demands extra fabric. To calculate the amount, measure the length of the pattern repeat by measuring the distance between the beginning of a pattern and the beginning of the next identical section. Add one of these lengths to the total amount for every width of fabric needed.

9 You will need to buy approximately the same amount of lining and interlining as for the curtains, minus any extra that has been added to the top fabric for matching patterns. (See individual instructions for any disparities in widths and lengths.) You will also need the same amount of heading tape as the heading width of your curtains and seam allowances at each side of 2.5 cm (1 in).

10 Allow extra fabric if you are adding ruffles and/or piping to curtains (see pages 142 and 141).

CUTTING OUT

You will need
Fabric
Lining (optional)
Interlining (optional)
Metre/yard stick
Set or L-square
Tailor's chalk

It is extremely important that curtain ends are cut

straight (the bottom and top edges must be at right angles to the selvedges). If the cross-wise threads (the weft) appear to be straight, cut into the selvedge and gently pull out a thread across the fabric. This will leave a clear cutting line.

If the crosswise grain doesn't appear to be straight, use a set or L-square to achieve a straight edge, lining up one corner of the set or L-square with the fabric selvedge. Alternatively use a sheet of newspaper, lining up an edge with the selvedge. Further sheets can then be pinned in position to give a straight line across the fabric.

Cut out curtain widths on a large table or clear an area of floor where you won't be disturbed. Check that you always cut printed fabric with the design running in the same direction. There are usually arrows on patterned furnishing fabric selvedges that indicate the top.

1 *Plain fabrics only.* Straighten the edge of the first curtain length by the methods mentioned above. Measure off the first length and, using a set or L-square and rule, mark a straight line across the curtain width with tailor's chalk. Cut, using long firm scissor strokes to prevent a ragged edge. Repeat to cut the remaining lengths.

2 Cut any half widths by folding the fabric in half lengthways, lining up the selvedges and then carefully cutting up the fold of the fabric.

3 To prevent puckering at the seams, cut off the selvedges if they are tightly woven. Otherwise snip into them at 5 cm (2 in) intervals to release the edges.

4 Repeat steps 1 to 3 for the optional lining and interlining.

5 *Patterned fabric lengths only.* Mark a straight line across the fabric where a row of design repeats begin. This will form the hem fold-line. Measure the length of the curtain up from this line and add the hem allowance below it (fig **2**). Cut across the fabric at the top and bottom of the curtain and

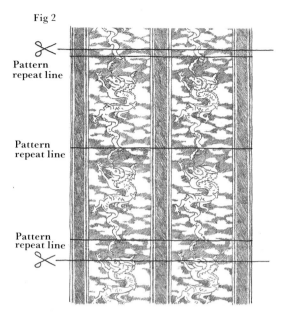

Fig 2

Pattern repeat line

Pattern repeat line

Pattern repeat line

identify the top end with a mark if necessary.

6 Locate the next line of pattern repeats. Draw a straight line across the fabric. Measure and cut the next curtain width as before, cutting away any waste material below the hem allowance. Continue until all the curtain lengths have been cut out.

UNLINED CURTAINS

You will need
Fabric
Heading tape
Matching thread

Making up
1 Refer to the measuring and cutting out sections and then cut out the curtain lengths. Stitch widths of fabric together if necessary to make up each curtain, positioning any half widths at the outer edge (fig **3**). Use a flat seam if stitching together selvedges or edges that can be neatly finished off. To hide raw edges use French seams (*see page 140*). Press.

2 If the fabric is patterned, it should be matched across seams. Press under the seam allowance along one of the edges to be joined and place it over the seam allowance of the other unfolded edge so that the pattern matches exactly (fig **4**). Pin in place. To make the pattern match exactly all

the way up the curtain, you may have to ease the fabric lengthways as you pin.

3 Next ladderstitch across the join (*see page 139*) and fold the fabric with right sides together. Stitch the fabric pieces together and neaten seams. Press. To conceal raw edges, use a flat fell seam (*see page 140*). The topstitching will be hidden by the pattern.

4 On both patterned and unpatterned curtains, press 6 mm ($\frac{1}{4}$ in) to the wrong side down the side edges

Fig 3

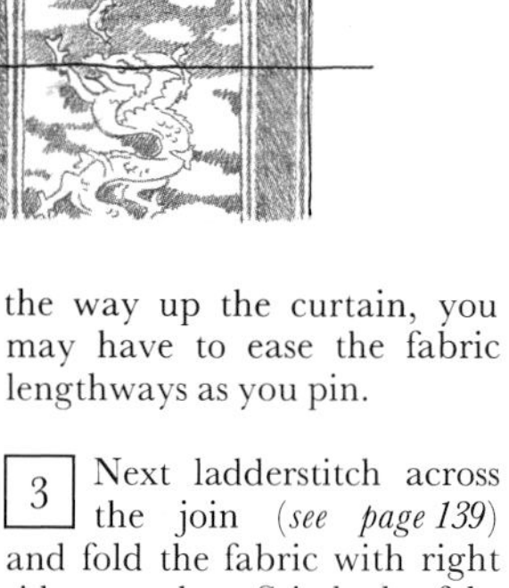

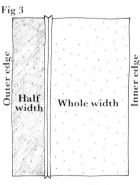

Outer edge

Half width

Whole width

Inner edge

Fig 4

of the curtain. Turn under 4.5 cm ($1\frac{3}{4}$ in), pin and press, leaving the bottom 10 cm (4 in) free. If you are using a sheer fabric, turn under 2.5 cm (1 in) then 2.5 cm (1 in) again to make a double hem down each side.

5 Turn up 5 cm (2 in) twice along the base to make a double hem and press, folding the corners into mitres (*see page 141*). Slipstitch (*see page 140*) the edges of the mitre together.

6 Slipstitch the hem in place along the base and sides of the curtain. Sheer fabrics look better machine stitched.

7 Measure off the finished length of the curtain from the base and mark a straight line across the curtain top. Press the excess fabric to the wrong side.

8 Cut a length of heading tape to the curtain width plus 10 cm (4 in). If you are using a pinch pleat heading check the positioning of the pleats when gathered up (*see page 99*) before you cut. If a triple or cartridge pleat falls at an edge you can cut the cords at the back to release.

9 At the tape end that will lie at the inner edge of the curtain, free the cords from the underside by 4 cm ($1\frac{1}{2}$ in) and knot. Trim the

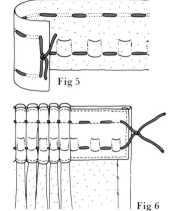

Pencil pleat heading tape

Fig 5

Fig 6

Pencil pleat heading tape attached to curtain

tape to within 6 mm ($\frac{1}{4}$ in) of the knots and turn under 1.5 cm ($\frac{5}{8}$ in) so the knots are at the back (fig 5). At the other end of the tape free the cords for 6.5 cm (2$\frac{1}{2}$ in) on the top side but do not knot. Trim the tape to within 12 mm ($\frac{1}{2}$ in) of the cords and turn under 6 mm ($\frac{1}{4}$ in).

10 With wrong sides together, line up the tape end with the loose cords against the outer curtain edge. Pin, then baste the tape to the curtain 3 mm ($\frac{1}{8}$ in) from the curtain top. Machine the heading tape to the curtain along all edges, being careful not to catch in the loose cords. Stitch both long edges in the same direction as this will prevent puckering while sewing.

11 Pull on the heading tape cords until the curtain is the correct width. Knot them neatly together, or wrap round a cord tidy (fig 6). Do not cut the cords as the heading will need to be released when the curtains are cleaned. Thread curtain hooks through the heading tape at about 7.5 cm (3 in) intervals with a hook positioned at each end.

RUFFLED CURTAINS WITH SEWN-IN LINING AND CONTRAST PIPING ON INNER EDGES

This method of sewing in a lining gives a neat finish down the curtain sides and is suitable for light- to medium-weight curtains. Should you wish to leave out the ruffles and piping, allow the usual amount (see step 1, measuring for curtains) for each side turning on the curtain fabric, but cut the lining 7 cm (2$\frac{3}{4}$ in) less than the *finished* curtain width. (The lining length remains the same as given below.) For binding on inner edge omit steps 3, 4 and 5 and insert steps 2, 3 and 5 of the bound tablecloth (*page 123*) after step 10.

You will need
Fabric inclusive of ruffle (see step 1 for ruffle fabric allowance)
Lining
Heading tape
Matching thread
Enough contrasting covered piping (*see page 141*) or

binding to equal the length of one side of the curtain plus 3 cm (1$\frac{1}{4}$ in)

Making up

1 Measure for the curtains (*see page 95*), this time allowing 2.5 cm (1 in) for each side turning. The lining should be equal to the *finished* curtain width and 7.5 cm (3 in) shorter than the unfinished length. Cut the curtain and lining lengths (*see page 95*). Cut a strip of fabric for the ruffle 17 cm (6$\frac{3}{4}$ in) wide times twice the finished length of the curtain plus 3 cm (1$\frac{1}{4}$ in). From the contrast fabric cut enough bias strips to equal the length of one side of the curtain when joined plus 3 cm (1$\frac{1}{4}$ in).

2 Stitch curtain and lining fabric widths together as necessary, matching patterned fabric across seams (see unlined curtains, step 2).

3 Fold the ruffle strip in half lengthways and turn in 1.5 cm ($\frac{5}{8}$ in) along the short ends. Slipstitch (*see page 140*) to close. Gather the ruffle (*see page 142*) to equal the finished curtain length.

4 With raw edges even, baste the piping to the ruffle, leaving loose ends of 1.5 cm ($\frac{5}{8}$ in) at the top and bottom to tuck in to the curtain seam allowance. To avoid bulky seams, push back the piping covering from these ends and cut away the cord.

5 Measure off the finished length of the curtain from the hem foldline, marking the hem and heading foldline on the *inner* side edge of the curtain. With raw edges even and unpiped side of the ruffle uppermost, baste the ruffle/piping section to the right side of the curtain fabric between the marked points, taking a 1.5 cm ($\frac{5}{8}$ in) seam allowance.

6 Lay the curtain flat, right side uppermost. Lay the lining over it, wrong side uppermost, matching the top and side raw edges. Stitch the lining to the curtain fabric down the sides to within 6.5 cm (2$\frac{1}{2}$ in) of the hem foldline, using a zipper foot when stitching the piped side (fig 7). As the lining is

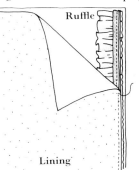

Fig 7   Piping

narrower than the curtaining, allow the top fabric to form slight folds beneath it.

7 Snip into the seam allowances at 10 cm (4 in) intervals. Turn the curtain right sides out. Press the inside ruffled seam so that it lies at the curtain edge. Now press the other side of the curtain; the top fabric will be drawn round to the wrong side, forming a 3 cm (1$\frac{1}{4}$ in) margin down the side edge.

8 Turn up 5 cm (2 in) twice along the base edge of the curtain to make a double hem, folding the hem diagonally at the unruffled corner and neatly covering the ruffle/piping seam allowances at the other side. Slipstitch the hem in place.

9 Turn up 2.5 cm (1 in) twice along the base edge of the lining. Press and machine stitch. Stitching on the underside of the lining, backstitch along the open part of the piped seam just above the hem to close. Slipstitch the remaining unstitched sections of the lining side edges to the curtain to finish.

10 Baste the lining to the curtain fabric along the top edge. Press the surplus fabric to the wrong side at the curtain top and attach the heading tape (see unlined curtains, steps 8 to 11).

CURTAINS WITH LOCKED-IN LINING

Lockstitching is a method of joining the curtain fabric and lining loosely together at intervals down the curtain length. It gives a professionally made look to large curtains and it helps them hang beautifully and evenly.

You will need
Fabric
Lining
Heading tape
Matching thread
Tailor's chalk
Metre/yard stick

Making up

1 Measure for the curtains and cut out curtain and lining widths (*see pages 95 and 96*). Cut the lining to the same width as the curtains, but 8 cm (3$\frac{1}{4}$ in) shorter in length.

2 Stitch together the curtain and then the lining widths, matching any pattern (see unlined curtains, step 2).

3 Press 5 cm (2 in) to the wrong side down each side of the curtain. Turn up and press a 10 cm (4 in) single hem along the base edge, folding mitred corners (*see page 141*). Slipstitch (*see page 140*) the edges of the mitres together.

4 Herringbone stitch (*see page 139*) along the raw side and hem base edges, picking up just a thread on the main fabric so the stitches will not show on the right side.

5 Curtain weights (*see page 95*) can be added to the base hem at this stage. Circular weights are stitched inside each mitre and at fabric joins (fig 8). Lengths of weighting are laid inside the hem and caught in place at evenly spaced intervals.

6 Lay the curtain out flat with the wrong side uppermost and begin marking the lockstitching rows. First, using a metre (yard) stick, mark down the centre of the curtain from the top to just above the hem edge. Working from this line outwards, mark parallel lines at about 30 cm (12 in) apart.

Fig 8

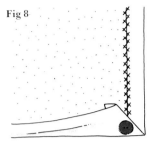

Fig 9

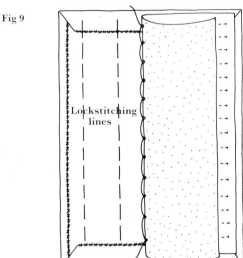

Lockstitching lines

7 With wrong sides facing, match the central line on the wrong side of the fabric with the centre of the lining. Pin the lining to the curtain fabric down the centre line and fold it back against the line of pins. Lockstitch (*see page 140*) the lining to curtain fabric beginning 10 cm (4 in) from the top raw edges and finishing 2.5 cm (1 in) from the curtain hem.

8 Pin the lining and curtain fabric together at the next marked line, then fold back the fabric and lockstitch together in the same way. Repeat at each marked line until the lockstitching is completed, working outwards both ways from the curtain centre (fig **9**).

9 Baste the lining and curtain fabric together at the top edge. Trim the lining at the sides to make it even with the edges of the curtain. Turn under the lining side edges for 2 cm ($\frac{3}{4}$ in) and press; turn under the hem edge for 4 cm ($1\frac{1}{2}$ in) and press, leaving a 2 cm ($\frac{3}{4}$ in) margin of fabric all round the curtain. Slipstitch

the lining to the turned-in edges of the curtain and along the hem. The stitches shouldn't come through to the right side of the curtain.

10 Turn down the top edges of the curtain the required amount and attach the heading tape (see unlined curtains, steps 8 to 11).

INTERLINED CURTAINS WITH HANDMADE TRIPLE PINCH PLEAT HEADING

For extra insulation and a sumptuous finish, add an interlining between the curtain fabric and the lining. This type of curtain always looks best with a handmade heading. A *cartridge pleat heading* can also be made by following the instructions below.

You will need
Fabric
Lining
Interlining
Matching thread
Buckram stiffening (the width of your heading)
Steel pin hooks or sew-on hooks (One hook for each pleat plus one for each edge)
Tailor's chalk
Curtain weights (optional)

Making up

1 Measure for the curtains and cut out curtain and lining widths (*see page 95*). The lining should be cut to the same width as the curtain but 8 cm ($3\frac{1}{4}$ in) less in length. Cut the interlining 10 cm (4 in) narrower and shorter than the curtain.

2 Stitch together the curtain and then the lining widths, matching any pattern (see unlined curtains, step 2).

3 To join widths of interlining, butt or slightly overlap the long edges and herringbone stitch (*see page 139*) together (fig **10**). You can also join widths with a machine zigzag stitch, but take care not to stretch the interlining when you do this.

4 Lay the curtain out flat, wrong side up and mark up for lockstitching (see curtains with locked-in lining, step 6). Place the interlining over the fabric, matching top edges, the curtain's side turnings and hem showing evenly all round. Lockstitch to the fabric as for lined curtains.

5 Baste the interlining to the fabric around the edges. Turn in the curtain sides 5 cm (2 in) and turn up hem edge 10 cm (4 in), folding mitred corners (*see page 141*). Slipstitch (*see page 140*) the edges of the mitre together. Curtain weights should be added at this stage if desired (see unlined curtains, step 6).

6 Leaving the depth of the buckram stiffening plus 10 cm (4 in) unstitched at the top of the curtain side edges, herringbone stitch down the side edges and along the hem. Make sure that the turnings are being stitched to the curtain fabric and not just the interlining.

7 Place the lining right side uppermost and matching central lockstitch line to the central point of the lining. Interlock the lining to the interlining as before, following the rows of stitching on the interlining as a guide if visible. Finish the stitching just above the hem. Fold back the lining from the curtain top.

8 Turn under the lining along the sides and base as for lined curtains, step 9, and slipstitch, leaving the heading allowance unstitched.

9 At the top of the curtain, turn the curtain fabric only to the wrong side by 3 cm ($1\frac{1}{4}$ in) and press. Trim the interlining to the foldline.

10 Slip the buckram underneath and below the curtain fabric turning so that its top edge matches the trimmed interlining foldline edge. Smooth the interlining over the buckram. Fold the curtain fabric over the interlining, mitring the corners (*see page 141*). Baste firmly in place through all thicknesses (except the lining) along the edges of the buckram, making sure this does not slip from under the top turning (fig **11a** and **b**)).

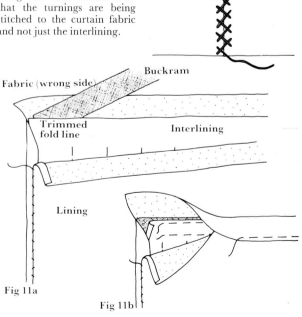

Fig 10

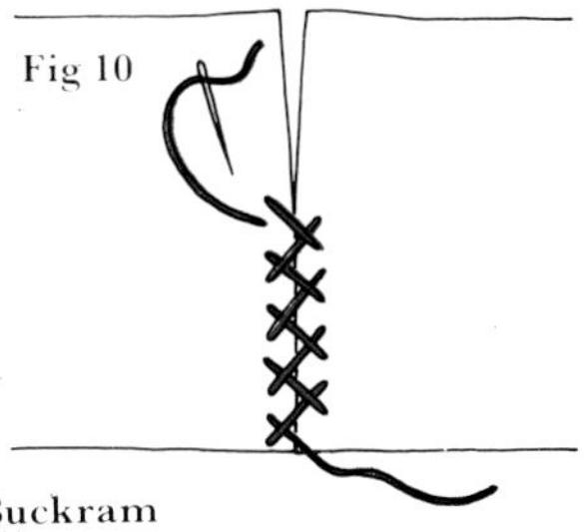

Buckram

Fabric (wrong side)

Trimmed fold line

Interlining

Lining

Fig 11a

Fig 11b

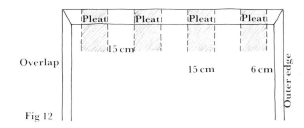

Fig 12

11 Turn in the top raw edge of the lining and slipstitch to the curtain 1 cm ($\frac{3}{8}$ in) below the top edge. Slipstitch the unstitched sections at the sides to close.

12 Next calculate the size and spacing of the pleats. You should have allowed two and a half times the track width in fabric for a triple pleat heading; this gives 10–15 cm (4–6 in) for each pleat, depending on the spaces between. See page 99 for notes on positioning pleats at outer and overlap edges of curtains. A width of 10 cm (4 in) makes a good fat cartridge pleat.

13 Decide approximately what width of spacing would look best on your curtains when they are made up. Fig **12** gives 15 cm (6 in) as an example. Next subtract half a flat section at each end, or the width of any overlap or return, from the *finished* width of the curtain (half the track length if you are dealing with a pair). Divide this figure by your proposed spacing width. The answer is the number of pleats that will fit across the curtain. The exact spacing width can then be found by dividing the finished curtain width (less end/overlap/return allowances) by the number of pleats less one.

14 To find out the width of each pleat, subtract the width measurement of the *finished* curtain from the width of the *flat* curtain and divide the answer by the proposed number of pleats.

15 Using a ruler or set or L-square, mark vertical lines to show the positions of the pleats on the wrong side of the curtain top.

16 Bring the two lines marking the first pleat together to form a single large pleat on the right side of the curtain. Pin, then baste down the pleat line to the lower edge of the stiffening, being careful to sew in a straight line. Repeat for each pleat. Machine or back stitch each pleat down the basting line through all thicknesses.

17 *Triple pleats only.* Working from the right side of the curtain, divide each pleat in three by folding concertina fashion. Just above the lower edge of the stiffening, backstitch several times through the base of each set of pleats to hold them in place. At the top edge of the curtain catch the pleats together at the back (fig **13**).

18 *Cartridge pleats only.* Working from the right side of the curtain, flatten each pleat gently and catch against the main fabric with a few handstitches placed each side of the pleat base just behind the fold. Pad the base of the pleat with cotton wool (batting) to give a softly rounded appearance.

19 Stab in pin hooks at the back of each set of pleats at the required depth, or sew on curtain hooks.

CASED HEADINGS

Curtains and valances can be hung by threading a pole, rod or length of wire through a channel sewn in the top of the curtain (*see page 94*)

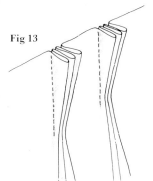

Fig 13

known as a casing. This method is particularly suitable for hanging curtains which won't be drawn and ones that hang in a recess or against a window.

QUICK CASING FOR LIGHTWEIGHT KITCHEN/BATHROOM CURTAIN

Making up

1 Allowing 12 cm (5 in) for the heading (this gives a 4 cm/1$\frac{1}{2}$ in frill), make up an unlined curtain following the instructions on page 96, steps 1 to 6. It should have a finished width of 1$\frac{1}{2}$ times the rod/wire length.

2 Turn 6 cm (2$\frac{1}{2}$ in) to the wrong side at the top of the curtain and press. Fold over 6 cm (2$\frac{1}{2}$ in) again. Stitch along the lower edge of the turning close to the fold. Then stitch another row 2.5 cm (1 in) above this first line of stitching. This forms the casing. If the curtain support is greater than 12 mm ($\frac{1}{2}$ in) in diameter, casing calculations have to be more detailed (see below).

FIXED CURTAINS WITH FABRIC-COVERED POLE

You will need
Fabric
Heading tape
Matching thread

Making up

1 Follow the instructions for making unlined curtains, steps 1 to 6, allowing for a finished width of 1$\frac{1}{2}$ times the length of the pole. Measure the curtain length from underneath the pole, adding a casing allowance of the pole circumference measurement plus 4 cm

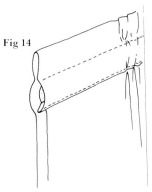

Fig 14

(1$\frac{1}{2}$ in) for ease, plus a further 11 cm (4$\frac{1}{2}$ in) for the ruffle.

2 When you have reached heading tape attachment stage, make the casing as follows. Fold over the curtain top by *half* the pole circumference plus 8 cm (3$\frac{1}{4}$ in). Press under the raw edges of the turning by 12 mm ($\frac{1}{2}$ in). Stitch across the curtain through all thicknesses close to the folded hem edge.

3 Stitch across the turning again, half the casing allowance plus 2 cm ($\frac{3}{4}$ in) above the first row of stitching to form the channel for the pole (fig **14**). *See page 139 for instructions on covering the pole.*

FIXED CURTAINS WITH CONTRAST-BOUND HEADING

You will need
Fabric
Contrast fabric for bound heading
Matching thread

Making up

1 Follow the instructions for making up unlined curtains, steps 1 to 6. Allow a finished width of 1$\frac{1}{2}$ times the length of the pole. To the curtain length (measured from under the pole) add a casing allowance of *half* the pole circumference measurement plus 1 cm ($\frac{3}{8}$ in) for ease plus a further 7.5 cm (3 in).

2 Cut a strip of contrast fabric that measures the width of the ungathered finished curtain plus 4 cm (1$\frac{1}{2}$ in) by a depth of half the pole circumference plus 1 cm ($\frac{3}{8}$ in) for ease, plus a further 10.5 cm (4$\frac{1}{4}$ in).

3 When heading tape attachment stage has been reached, make the casing. Turn in 1 cm ($\frac{3}{8}$ in) twice at the ends of the contrast strip to make double hems. Slipstitch. With right sides together, raw edges even, stitch the contrast strip to the curtain top, taking a 1.5 cm ($\frac{5}{8}$ in) seam allowance.

4 Fold the contrast strip over the seam allowance to the wrong side of the curtain, leaving a 1.5 cm ($\frac{5}{8}$ in) margin of binding on the right side (fig **15**). Press.

Fig 15

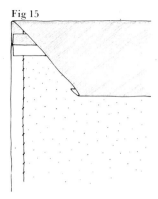

Fig 16

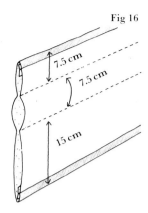

5 Turn under 1.5 cm ($\frac{5}{8}$ in) along the raw edge of the strip and press. Stitch across the curtain, close to the lower fold.

6 Stitch across the curtain again half the pole circumference plus 1 cm ($\frac{3}{8}$ in) above the first row of stitching to make the casing for the pole. Slipstitch (*see page 140*) the edges of the casing together above the pole to neaten if desired.

COMBINED CURTAIN AND VALANCE

The valance shown in this bathroom is fed onto a pole in exactly the same way as a cased heading, but since it has a lower, bound ruffle, the making up method is different from that employed for a lined, cased heading previously described.

Here the lining extends below the pole and is wrapped around the bottom edge of the valance to form the binding. The lining therefore doubles as the contrast chintz.

You will need
Fabric
Contrast lining fabric
Matching thread

Making up
1 To calculate the measurements, measure the width of the pole to be used, and multiply by 1$\frac{1}{2}$, adding 2.5 cm (1 in) at each end for seam allowances to make a total of 5 cm (2 in). (The curtains, when finished and in their flat state, are attached behind the flat valance, beginning at each outer edge. They are also calculated as being 1$\frac{1}{2}$ times the width of the pole, although they are of course fixed, and will not be drawn. See step 11 below.)

2 Calculate the depth of the valance required. In the example featured here a full depth of 30 cm (12 in) has been allowed, exclusive of seam allowances, and is made up as follows of 7.5 cm (3 in) for the top ruffle, 7.5 cm (3 in) for the pole (calculated as 12 cm (5 in) in circumference plus 2.5 cm (1 in) ease allowance—a total of 15 cm (6 in); see Cased Headings), and a larger, 15 cm (6 in) ruffle below the pole.

The contrast lining fabric will therefore amount to a depth of 30 cm (12 in) plus binding and seam allowances (1.5 cm ($\frac{5}{8}$ in) × 2, plus 1.5 cm ($\frac{5}{8}$ in) × 2 = 6 cm (2$\frac{1}{2}$ in), making a total of 36 cm (14$\frac{1}{2}$ in)). See fig **16**.

3 Cut two straight grain lengths of fabric, one of print and one of contrast lining fabric, following your measurements for each strip, and taking account of the position of any print you may wish to feature.

4 Place fabric against contrast lining, right sides together and matching raw edges at the top only. Pin along the length of the valance at the top, basting if necessary, then stitch from one side to the other, 1.5 cm ($\frac{5}{8}$ in) in from raw edges. Press seam allowances open.

5 Repeat step 4 for the remaining long raw edges of the valance, to form a tube. Turn.

6 With right side of valance uppermost, fold back a binding allowance of 1.5 cm ($\frac{3}{8}$ in) at the top of the valance to the wrong side, and press all along the top edge to set. Flattening the valance tube on the ironing

board, right side uppermost, repeat this operation to form the lower bound edge of the valance.

7 At each short end of the valance, turn in 2.5 cm (1 in) to the inside of the tube, pin, baste from top to bottom and press.

8 Keeping the valance right side uppermost, measure down 7.5 cm (3 in) from the top folded edge of the binding, and mark all along the length of the valance with a line of pins or basting. Stitch along this line from end to end to form the first casing line. Measure a further 7.5 cm (3 in) down from this stitching line, and marking with pins, stitch a second line all along the length of the valance.

9 At each short end of valance, slipstitch from the top to the first casing stitch line, and from the bottom to the second casing stitch line.

10 Unpick basting stitches at each end of the casing channel, and press to finish.

To attach the valance to the curtains
11 The curtains, which are lined but not stiffened or interlined, are measured in the normal way described in the section on curtains with locked-in lining (*see page 97*), from just under the pole. Calculate 1$\frac{1}{2}$ times the width of the pole for the curtains, so that they match the valance, plus all extra seam allowances and lining details as referred to in that section.

The curtains should be fixed to the valance at exactly

the same spot as that from which they were measured i.e. from just underneath the pole, and they should therefore be attached just below the second casing stitch line. Since they are fixed and do not need to be closed, you will find that they take about half the length of the pole in total, while the valance takes up the remaining half-length, situated in the middle of the pole.

12 Set curtains flat, laying the valance over their tops so that the top of each curtain comes parallel and just under, the casing's lower stitch line, and each curtain is positioned so that its outer edge comes level with the valance's outer edge. See fig **17**. Pin, baste and stitch from each outer edge of the valance and through the curtain thickness to the inner edge of each curtain. (If the curtains seem heavy, make a double row of stitching 1 cm ($\frac{3}{8}$ in) down from the first line, to strengthen.) Press to finish.

CURVED VALANCE WITH RUFFLED, PIPED EDGE

The valance shown in this kitchen is really a short curtain, but since the technique of making it up comes closer to a combination of valance and cased heading, it has been included in this section.

PLEASE NOTE that here the pole has been calculated as being 10 cm (4 in) in diameter.

You will see from fig **18** below that the fabric and lining for the main section of the valance are of the same length. The double, bound ruffle is made up first of all,

Fig 17

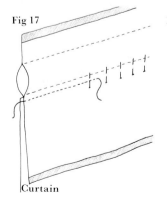

Curtain

Fig 18

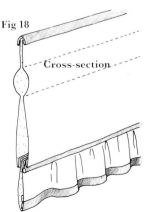

Cross-section

then set between lining and fabric like a sandwich filling together with the piping. The last part of the making up procedure is to set the casing stitches for the pole.

You will need
Fabric
Contrast fabric for binding and
**   piping**
Pre-shrunk piping cord
Lining
Cardboard
String
Pattern paper
Matching thread

Cutting the pattern for the valance

1 To calculate the width of the valance, multiply by $1\frac{1}{2}$ times the width of the pole, plus 2.5 cm (1 in) at each end for seam allowance, or a total of 5 cm (2 in).

2 To decide on the depth and shaping of the hemline you should make a template in cardboard or heavyweight brown paper, half the width of the pole, and deeper than the deepest shaped point of the valance. Divide the template into three equal sections, and mark in the vertical dividing lines from top to bottom. The valance shown here was a total depth beneath the pole of 38 cm (15 in), so mark in this measurement at the outer side of the template, and draw a line across the template 15 cm (6 in) down from the top. Make a small hole in each top corner of the template, then attach it to the pole with string so that its top is set directly under the pole. See fig **19**.

3 You will notice from the picture of the valance featured here that the ruffle dips in the section nearest to the centre of the window by roughly 5 cm (2 in) further than its position at the middle section, dropping sharply to a point in the centre of the third section nearest to the outer edge of the pole, to a depth of 38 cm (15 in). See fig **20**. Mark this curving line in on your template, then cut along this line so that you can check the depth of the valance with ruffle, against the light of the window. Adjust if necessary.

4 Remove the template. Because the ruffle ac-

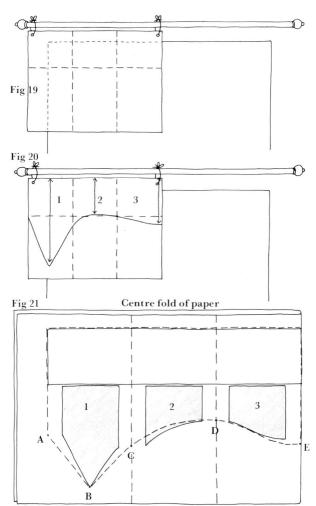

Fig 19

Fig 20

Fig 21　　　Centre fold of paper

1　2　3

A
B　C　D　E

Valance shape *minus* seam allowances

counts for the bottom 7.5 cm (3 in), draw a line this amount up from the bottom curved line and trim off. This template now forms the basis of the valance pattern, for pole to piping measurement.

5 Make a pattern of this half-shape by firstly folding a large sheet of pattern paper in half lengthwise, then marking it with a rectangle which measures 15 cm (6 in) deep (that is, to the bottom of the pole position), by the total width of the valance minus side seam allowances, and divided by half. (Decorator's lining paper is useful here because of its length.) Mark this rectangle into three equal vertical sections, continuing the lines downwards to the bottom of the paper.

6 Cut through the template at each vertical line to divide it into three parts, marking each part 1, 2 and 3. See fig **20**. Set

each of these marked sections squarely in the centre of each section on the paper pattern, lining the top of each section up with the under-pole position marked on the paper. Pin or weight the template sections firmly so they will not move, then mark in points A, B, C, D and E as marked on fig **21**, and draw a new line on the pattern paper joining A to E, to form the curve required.

7 Remove the template sections. Add seam allowances of 1.5 cm ($\frac{5}{8}$ in) to the curved bottom and to the top of the pattern, and 2.5 cm (1 in) at the outside edge of the pattern. Mark the central fold position on your pattern, and cut it out.

8 To calculate the ruffle, measure the bottom of the curved valance seamline, minus seam allowances, and double for the finished width of the ruffle. Double this measurement again for the

length of fabric needed for the ruffle and add seam allowances of 1.5 cm ($\frac{5}{8}$ in). Calculating a depth of 7.5 cm (3 in), cut a strip of fabric, allowing for joins if necessary, of the above measurements. For the lining, multiply the length above by a depth of 10.5 cm ($4\frac{1}{4}$ in) and cut this out, again allowing for joins and seam allowances as above.

9 For the binding at the top of the valance cut a strip of contrast fabric the complete width of the valance plus its seam allowances at each end (see step 1), by 6 cm ($2\frac{1}{2}$ in) deep.

10 For piping, cut strips of contrast fabric to measure the same length as in step 9, but 3 cm ($1\frac{1}{4}$ in) wide only. These must be cut on the bias. Join bias strips and piping (*see page 141*).

11 Lastly, cut out the valance and lining as one, using the valance pattern and laying one piece of fabric over the other, and allowing for joins where necessary (don't forget 3 cm ($1\frac{1}{4}$ in) total seam allowances for each join). Remember to allow extra fabric for print matching, if necessary.

Making up

12 Firstly, make up the ruffle. Set lower long edge of fabric and contrast lining of ruffle right sides together, matching raw edges, and pin. Stitch along complete length of ruffle, from side to side, 1.5 cm ($\frac{5}{8}$ in) in from raw edges. Press seam allowances open, then fold contrast lining over to wrong side of fabric so that remaining raw edges of fabric and contrast lining come together, with their right sides outside. Press the fold formed, which will then also form the bound edge of the ruffle.

Fold in short ends of ruffle strip to inside at seam allowance points, 1.5 cm ($\frac{5}{8}$ in) in from the edge, and slipstitch (*see page 140*) to close. Run two lines of gathering stitches along complete length of remaining raw edges of ruffle, 1.5 cm ($\frac{5}{8}$ in) and 1 cm ($\frac{3}{8}$ in) in from edges respectively, breaking gathering stitches at equal intervals to make gathering-up easier.

Gather up ruffle to match measurement of lower curved edge of valance, and stitch along the central point of these two gathering lines from end to end, to set ruffle.

13 To make up piping, take a length of pre-shrunk piping cord equal to the joined, contrast bias strip and wrap the length of the bias around the cord, right side of bias outside and matching raw edges. Stitch along the length of the wrapped cord, close to its edge, using the piping or zipper foot on your machine. Trim seam allowances to 1.5 cm ($\frac{5}{8}$ in), see fig 22.

14 Taking up valance fabric and lining, press 2.5 cm (1 in) to the wrong side at each short end of the valance. Set aside valance lining, and laying valance fabric right side uppermost, set piping along its lower curved edge, right sides together and matching raw edges, curving the piping off at each side foldback point, 1.5 cm ($\frac{5}{8}$ in) up from the raw edge. See figs 23a) and b). Pin, baste, and stitch from end to end, stitching through piping at each folded-in edge of valance fabric as shown in fig 23b). Slash through piping seam allowance at pointed corners to ease.

15 Set right side of ruffle i.e. with its bound edge facing downwards against the valance, against right side of valance fabric and piping, with its raw edges matching those of the valance and piping, and its outside slip-stitched edges matching the pressed in edges of the valance. Stitch from end to end, 1.5 cm ($\frac{5}{8}$ in) in from matching raw edges. See fig 24. Slash through seam allowances to stitching line at valance corner to ease. Trim seam allowances of ruffle to 1 cm ($\frac{3}{8}$ in) to eliminate any unnecessary bulk.

16 Set curved edge of valance lining against curved, piped and ruffled edge of valance fabric, right sides together and matching raw edges, so that piping and ruffle form a sandwich filling between lining and valance fabric. See fig 25. Pin into posi-

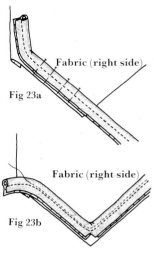

Fig 22

Fig 23a Fabric (right side)

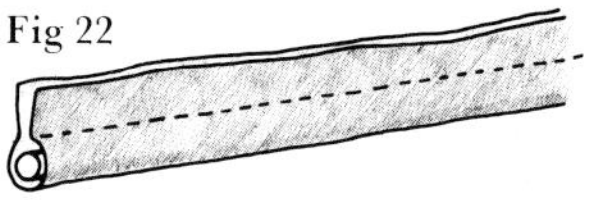

Fig 23b Fabric (right side)

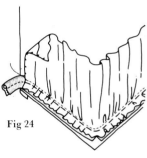

Fig 24

Fig 25

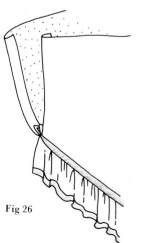

Fig 26

tion, matching folded-in sides of valance, baste, then stitch from side to side, through all thicknesses and 1.5 cm ($\frac{5}{8}$ in) in from raw edges. Trim lining fabric seam allowance to 1 cm ($\frac{3}{8}$ in) and clip curves.

17 Turn valance so that lining fabric folds to the back and the ruffle and piping are now visible at the curved lower edge of the valance. Press very carefully. See fig 26.

18 To prepare the valance for its final top ruffle binding, set top raw edges of both lining and valance fabric together and baste from one side to the other. Set one long edge of the binding against the valance fabric, right sides together and matching raw edges, turning in 2.5 cm (1 in) seam allowance at each end. Pin, then stitch from side to side. Press seam allowances open. Fold back 1.5 cm ($\frac{5}{8}$ in) at the remaining raw, long edge of the binding to the wrong side and press. Set this folded edge to the wrong side of the valance, so that the fold lies directly on top of the stitching line just made. Slipstitch along the length of the binding to attach to the lining. The ruffle binding will then be automatically formed at the top of the valance. Press flat carefully to set.

19 To form valance casing, set the valance right side uppermost, flat in front of you. Measuring down from the top of the binding to a depth of 7.5 cm (3 in), mark a line along the length of the valance parallel with the top, with pins, then mark a further parallel line 6 cm ($2\frac{1}{2}$ in) below this first line. Stitch along both pinned lines from end to end of the valance and through the lining, to form the casing for the pole. Slipstitch down each side of the valance, from the top to the first line of casing stitching, and from the second line of casing stitching to the bias point. Your valance is now complete.

SWAGS AND TAILS (JABOTS) FOR A BAY WINDOW

These look best against long windows in a room with a high ceiling. The ones shown on page 59 feature a central stripe in the print and the swags are cut on the length-ways grain so that this stripe will fall correctly. Both swags and tails (jabots) are lined. They are attached to a pelmet (cornice) board fixed to the wall. See fig 27.

You will need
Fabric for the swags, small and large tails (jabots), small and large tail (jabot) linings
Lining for the swags and small tails (jabots)
A weighted cord or chain
Pattern paper
Staple gun
Tailor's chalk

Cutting the pattern for the swag
1 Measure the width of the pelmet (cornice).

2 Decide how deep your swag should drape in the middle. As a guide it should be about one sixth of the curtain length.

3 Take a length of heavy cord or a chain and fix at one side of the pelmet (cornice) at the depth you would like the sides of the swag to finish. Let the cord drop in a gentle curve and fix at the other side of the pelmet (cornice). The length of this curve will equal the bottom edge of the swag.

4 Make a paper pattern for the swag as follows. Draw a rectangle measuring the width of the pelmet (cornice) by double the swag centre depth. Add 5 cm (2 in) to the top of the rectangle to allow for foldback over the pelmet (cornice) shelf. Mark the corners of this rectangle A, B, C and D. To achieve the curve at the bottom of the swag, subtract the C-D measurement from the chain length measurement, and add half this amount at each side of the square base, extending it to E and F. Join the outer points A and E, B and F (fig 28). Add a seam allowance of 1.5 cm ($\frac{5}{8}$ in) to the sides and base edge and cut out the pattern.

Making up
5 Cut out the number of swags you need plus the lining sections, making allowances for any print to be featured.

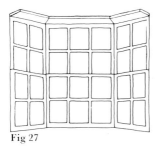

Fig 27

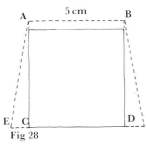

Fig 28

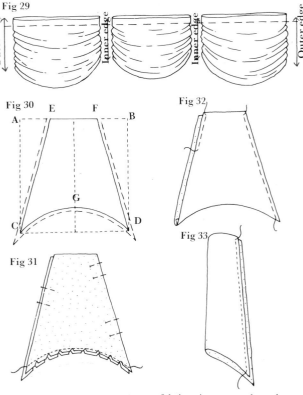

Fig 29

Fig 30

Fig 31

Fig 32

Fig 33

6 With right sides together and raw edges even, stitch each swag piece to each lining section, leaving the top edge of the swag open. Trim the corners and turn to the right side. Press, then matching the top raw edges, stitch across to hold.

7 Divide the swag into evenly spaced pleats at each side, drawing it up to the required depth and ending the pleating 5 cm (2 in) from the top (fig 29). The pleats should face upwards. Baste each pleat in place. Pin each swag against the side of a table to check that the pleat falls evenly and smoothly. Sew each pleat in place by hand. Repeat for the other two swags, attach central swag to two side swags with loose hand stitches and set aside.

Small central tails (jabots)

8 Draw a rectangle 40.5 cm (16 in) across by 56 cm (22 in) deep, marking corners A, B, C and D. Draw a line from top to bottom, through the centre of the rectangle. Mark a point G, 15 cm (6 in) up from the bottom of this line, and join CGD in a curved line. On line AB, mark in points 12.5 cm (5 in) from each side, marking them E and F. Join EC and FD.

9 Add 1 cm ($\frac{3}{8}$ in) seam allowances all round ECGD and F and 5 cm (2 in) along EF, and cut out along this line. See fig 30.

To make up

10 Cut out four fabric pieces from the pattern, matching prints if necessary. Mark two pieces and make up as linings.

11 With right sides together and matching raw edges, join a lining to a fabric piece and stitch around curved bottom line CD, 1 cm ($\frac{3}{8}$ in) in from raw edges. Clip seam allowance curves all along this line, turn and press. See fig 31.

12 Baste diagonal sides of lining and fabric wrong sides together, raw edges matching, then folding in half lengthways, right sides together, stitch from top to bottom, 1 cm ($\frac{3}{8}$ in) in from raw edges. See figs 32 and 33. Neaten seam allowance, turning up lower pointed end to conceal with a few handstitches.

Cutting the pattern for the large side tails (jabots)

13 Decide on the depth of the tail (jabot) at the side and inner edges. As a guide the side edge is equal to twice the depth of the finished swag and the inner edge is equal to the finished depth. However this depends on the effect you want to create and the proportions of the window or the curtains beneath.

14 To calculate tail width, add the width of the pelmet (cornice) return (the side of the pelmet) to the desired width of the folded part of the tail (jabot). This should cover the pleated edges of the swag by about 23 cm (9 in), but this varies according to taste and the width of the pelmet (cornice).

15 On a large sheet of pattern paper draw fig 34 to the scale indicated, marking in the pleat fold and placement lines and the width of the pelmet (cornice) return. Add 5 cm (2 in) to the top to allow for foldback over the pelmet (cornice) shelf and a seam allowance of 1.5 cm ($\frac{5}{8}$ in) on the other three edges. The pattern can be pleated following the instructions in step 20 below and pinned to

the pelmet (cornice) board to check the effect. Adjustments can then be made to the pattern before cutting out.

Making up

16 Cut out the tail and lining pieces, reversing the pattern to cut the second piece (otherwise you will have two right-hand tails/jabots) matching points and transferring the markings on to the right side of the lining pieces. Separate the cut-out pieces into left- and right-hand tails (jabots).

17 With right sides together and raw edges even, stitch the tail (jabot) and lining

fabric pieces together down the sides and across the diagonal edge, leaving the top edge open. Trim the corners, turn and press. Baste the raw edges of each tail together across the top.

18 Next pleat each tail (jabot). Beginning at the inner edge, fold the tail (jabot) at the first foldline and bring it over to the following placement line. Pin in place. Repeat until you have three pleats. See fig 35.

19 Baste across the pleats at the top to hold. Set against the pelmet (cornice) to check the positioning of the

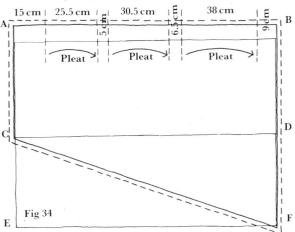

Fig 34

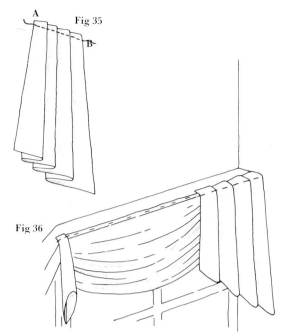

Fig 35

Fig 36

pleats. Adjust if necessary, then take down the tail (jabot) and stitch across the top of the pleated tail (jabot) 6 mm ($\frac{1}{4}$ in) from the raw edges. Stitch across again 6 mm ($\frac{1}{4}$ in) below the previous row of stitches.

Positioning swags and tails (jabots)

20 Staple each swag in place, overlapping the pelmet (cornice) shelf by 5 cm (2 in).

21 Place a small tail (jabot) over each swag join, lining up top raw edges. Staple in place. Catch the back of each tail (jabot) loosely to the folds of the swags so they fall naturally.

22 Position each large tail (jabot) at the edges of the pelmet (cornice), clipping into the foldback allowance at the

pelmet (cornice) corners if the angle is sharp. (On page 58 the returns have been angled to fit the bay.) Staple in place. See fig **36**.

SWAG AND CONTRAST-LINED TAILS (JABOTS)

The swag and tails (jabots) on page 88 are made in plain fabric to emphasize their sculpted folds. They have been constructed in exactly the same way as in the previous instructions, but the tails (jabots) have one more pleat and both swag and tails (jabots) have been finished with tape along the top edges. The lower edge of the swag is also cut curved rather than straight. The swag fabric and lining can be cut along the length of the fabric to eliminate width joins if the swag is very wide.

The curtains shown with the swag and tails (jabots) are lined with the same contrasting glazed cotton as the tails and are interlined for warmth and drape.

You will need
Fabric for the swag and two tails (jabots)
Contrasting lining for the above
Enough 2.5 cm (1 in) wide tape to neaten the top edge of the swag and finished tails (jabots)
Staple gun
Heavy cord or a chain
Pattern paper
Tailor's chalk

Cutting the pattern for the swag
1 Repeat the instructions for swags and tails (jabots) for a bay window, steps 1 to 3.

2 Make a paper pattern for the swag as follows. Draw a rectangle measuring the width of the pelmet (cornice) by double the swag centre depth. Add 5 cm (2 in) to the top of the rectangle to allow for foldback over the pelmet (cornice) shelf. Mark the corners of this rectangle A, B, C and D. Fold the pattern in half lengthways and crease. Unfold.

3 Subtract C-D from the measurement of the curve and add half this amount at each end of the rectangle base, extending it to E and F. Subtract double the side depth from the centre depth measurement. Measure this distance from the corners E, F and mark G, H. Join these points with a curved line that touches C-D at the crease. Add a seam allowance of 1.5 cm ($\frac{5}{8}$ in) to the side and base edges. Cut out the pattern.

Making up
4 Make up the swag following the previous instructions, steps 5 to 7, clipping curved edge before turning to the right side.

5 Baste the fabric and lining together at the top of the swag. Stitch a length of tape across the top to strengthen, matching the outer edge of the tape with the raw edges of the swag. Sew the tape along all edges.

6 Use a staple gun along the taped edge to fix the swag, overlapping the pelmet (cornice) shelf by 5 cm (2 in).

Cutting the pattern for tails (jabots)
7 Follow the previous instructions, steps 13 to 15. The cutting plan shown in fig **34** should be amended as follows. To accommodate the extra pleat, the depth at the side should be two and a half times the depth of the finished swag at the centre and the inner edge should be three quarters the finished depth (*see page 103*). The top edge of the tail (jabot) should measure the pelmet (cornice) return plus four times the width of the pleated section of the tail (jabot).

Making up
8 Follow the previous instructions, steps 16 to 19, making four pleats rather than three. Stitch tape across the tail (jabot) top as before.

9 Staple each tail (jabot) in place, overlapping the top of the pelmet (cornice) by 5 cm (2 in) and clipping diagonally into the corner allowance.

PELMETS (CORNICES)

A fabric pelmet (cornice) gives a decorative finish to the tops of curtains; it can change the proportions of a window, and hide an unattractive curtain track. As a general rule between one sixth and one eighth of the curtain drop is considered a suitable depth for a pelmet (cornice), but obviously this varies according to taste and individual windows.

The pelmets (cornices) in this section consist of three layers: a top fabric and lining which are each bonded to a middle layer of double-sided adhesive stiffener and slip-stitched together around the edges. They are then fixed to a shelf, the pelmet (cornice) board, over the window, using Velcro.

If widths of fabric have to be joined, place the full width of fabric in the middle of the pelmet (cornice) and narrow panels at either side. Match patterns across seams (page 139, Ladderstitch).

THE PELMET (CORNICE) BOARD

This is a length of plywood 1.5 to 2 cm ($\frac{5}{8}$ to $\frac{3}{4}$ in) thick by 10 cm (4 in) wide. Position it just above the curtain track or window frame using small metal brackets set about 30 cm (12 in) apart and placing a bracket at each end of the board (fig 1). The board should extend at least 5 cm (2 in) either side of the curtain track. It should be rounded at the outer corners to soften the line. Before fixing the board to the wall brackets, glue the hooked half of a strip of Velcro to the sides of the board (fig 2).

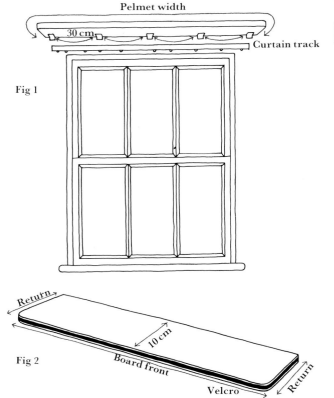

Pelmet width

30 cm

Curtain track

Fig 1

Fig 2 — Return, 10 cm, Board front, Velcro, Return

PELMET (CORNICE) WITH PIPING AND DOUBLE RUFFLE

The stiffened part of the pelmet (cornice) and ruffle shown on page 80 are of equal 10 cm (4 in) depth. This looks best over short curtains.

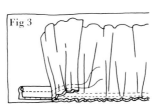

Fig 3

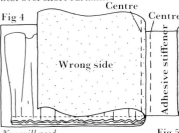

Fig 4 — Wrong side — Centre — Centre — Adhesive stiffener — Backing paper

Fig 5 — Fold over — Adhesive stiffener

You will need
Fabric
Curtain lining sateen
Contrast fabric for piping bias strips (*see page 141*)
Pre-shrunk piping cord
Double-sided adhesive stiffener for pelmet (cornice)
Velcro

Measuring and cutting out

1. Read through the notes at the beginning of the section. Decide on the overall depth of the pelmet (cornice) and ruffle and how deep each should be. To find the finished width of the pelmet (cornice), measure the front edge of the board (fig **2**) and add 20 cm (8 in) for the returns (the board ends).

2. For the pelmet (cornice), cut or make up one piece of fabric and one piece of lining to the finished width plus 3 cm ($1\frac{1}{4}$ in) by the depth plus 3 cm ($1\frac{1}{4}$ in). Cut one piece of stiffening to the finished width and depth only with no allowances for turnings.

3. Cut out enough ruffle strips, measuring twice the desired depth plus 3 cm ($1\frac{1}{4}$ in), to equal twice the width of the pelmet (cornice) when joined. Allow 1.5 cm ($\frac{5}{8}$ in) on each strip end for joins.

4. Cut out enough bias strips from the contrast fabric to cover the required amount of piping cord when joined.

Making up

5. Cover the piping cord (*see page 141*) with the contrast bias strip. With raw edges even pin the piping to the right side of the top fabric piece along the lower long side edge. Pull back the covering at both ends, and snip away the cord for 1.5 cm ($\frac{5}{8}$ in). This avoids bulky turnings. Baste the piping in place.

6. Make up the double ruffle (*see page 142*), breaking the gathering stitches at intervals if necessary and leaving a seam allowance of 1.5 cm ($\frac{5}{8}$ in) at the ends. Turn in the ends and slipstitch (*see page 140*) to close. With raw edges even, apply ruffle (*see page 142*) to the right side of the lower edge of the pelmet over the piping, positioning the ends of the ruffle 1.5 cm ($\frac{5}{8}$ in) in from the pelmet (cornice) ends and adjusting the gathers evenly (fig **3**). Stitch in place through all thicknesses, using the zipper foot on the machine.

7. Lay the stiffening flat. At the centre carefully cut the backing paper across the width. Peel back the paper a little way on either side and, matching centres, place the wrong side of the fabric over the exposed area of adhesive, the fabric turning allowances overlapping at either side by 1.5 cm ($\frac{5}{8}$ in) (fig **4**). Continue peeling back the paper while smoothing the fabric on to the adhesive, working from the

centre outwards so the fabric does not wrinkle. Set aside.

8 Fold under the edges of the lining to the wrong side by 1.5 cm ($\frac{5}{8}$ in). Press. Baste across the corners to hold. Stitch the soft half of the Velcro strip along the top of the lining so that the pelmet (cornice) will just cover the edge of the board when it is fixed in place.

9 Removing the backing paper as you work, fold the top fabric edges to the wrong side of the pelmet (cornice), smoothing them down on to the adhesive surface (fig **5**) and mitring corners (see page 141). This will bring the piping and ruffle down to the lower edge.

10 Working from the centre outwards, stick the wrong side of the lining to the wrong side of the pelmet (cornice), matching edges on all sides. Slipstitch (see page 140) the lining and fabric together around the edges.

11 Matching Velcro strips, press the pelmet (cornice) in place to hang.

PIPED PELMET (CORNICE) WITH LINED CONTRAST-EDGED RUFFLE

This is a variation of the ruffled pelmet (cornice) above, but the pelmet (cornice) has shrunk to a 5 cm (2 in) band. It is piped along both long edges and the ruffle is lined with contrasting fabric that extends round the edges to form a binding. It can be gathered by hand or you can apply standard heading tape. The pelmet (cornice) can be lined with ordinary curtain sateen.

You will need
Fabric
Contrast lining for ruffle and pelmet (cornice)
Contrast fabric for piping bias strips (see page 141)
Pre-shrunk piping cord
2.5 cm (1 in) wide standard heading tape (optional)
Velcro
Double-sided adhesive stiffener for pelmet (cornice)

Measuring and cutting out
1 Read through the general notes on pelmets (cornices) at the beginning of

the section. For the pelmet (cornice) cut one piece of fabric and one piece of lining that measures 8 cm ($3\frac{1}{4}$ in) wide by the length of the board front plus returns (fig **2**) plus 3 cm ($1\frac{1}{4}$ in). Cut a piece of stiffener that measures 5 cm (2 in) wide by the length of the board front plus returns (the finished dimensions of the pelmet/cornice).

2 For the ruffle cut or make up a strip of top fabric that measures the desired depth plus 1.5 cm ($\frac{5}{8}$ in) by twice the finished width of the pelmet (cornice). Match any pattern across seams (see page 139) as necessary. Cut or make up one strip of contrast lining that measures the desired ruffle depth plus 3.5 cm ($1\frac{3}{8}$ in) by twice the finished width of pelmet (cornice).

3 Cut out enough bias strips from the contrast fabric to cover the required amount of piping cord.

Making up
4 Follow step 5 of the previous instructions to apply the piping. It is attached to both long edges of the pelmet (cornice) front.

5 With raw edges even and right sides together, stitch the contrast lining and ruffle top fabric together along the long lower edge, taking a 1 cm ($\frac{3}{8}$ in) seam allowance. Press the seam open. Turn to the right side. Pin the top raw edges together and press the ruffle; the lining will form a 1 cm ($\frac{3}{8}$ in) margin on the right side lower edge.

Fig 6

Fig 7

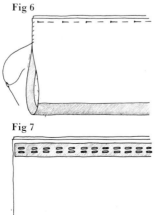

6 Turn in the ends of the ruffle to the wrong side by 1.5 cm ($\frac{5}{8}$ in) and slipstitch (see page 140) to close (fig **6**).

7 If you wish to gather the ruffle with standard heading tape, stitch it (see page 96) to the lined side of the ruffle with the top of the row of slots lying 2 cm ($\frac{3}{4}$ in) down from the raw edges

(fig **7**). Otherwise gather the ruffle in the usual way (see page 142).

8 Gather the ruffle and attach to the pelmet (cornice) as in step 6 of the previous instructions, taking a 1.5 cm ($\frac{5}{8}$ in) seam allowance. Tie the cord ends in a knot if using tape. Complete as for steps 7 to 11 of the previous instructions.

TIEBACKS

MEASURING UP

To calculate where to place the tieback and how long it should be, loop a fabric tape measure around the curtain roughly two-thirds down and arrange the curtain into the curve or folds you want. The length on the tape measure gives you the finished tieback length. Mark the walls at the correct position for the tieback hook. The depth of the tieback varies. As a rough guide the tiebacks on sill-length curtains should be no more than 10 cm (4 in) deep, but sweeping floor-length curtains can take a proportionally greater depth.

Fig 1a

Fig 1b

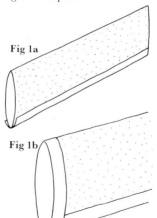

Fig 2

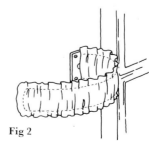

RUFFLED CASING FOR METAL ARM

You will need
Fabric
Matching thread

Measuring and cutting out
1 For each casing cut one piece of fabric that measures twice the length of the arm plus 2 cm ($\frac{3}{4}$ in) for seams by double the arm width plus 4.5 cm ($1\frac{3}{4}$ in) for seams and ease.

Making up
2 With wrong sides out, fold each strip in half lengthways so the long raw edges match. Pin and stitch the long raw edges of each casing strip together to make a tube, taking a 1 cm ($\frac{3}{8}$ in) seam allowance. Press the seam open. With the folded edge uppermost, stitch across the right-hand end of one of the casings, taking the same seam allowance as before (fig **1a**). Repeat the process on the other casing, with the seamed edge uppermost. (This means the seamed edge will be at the bottom on both right- and left-hand arms). Trim the corners.

3 Turn in 1 cm ($\frac{3}{8}$ in) twice at the open end of each casing. Stitch all the way round the opening to secure the turning (fig **1b**). Turn to the right side and press.

4 Beginning to one side of the opening, stitch along one long edge, around the closed end and along the other long edge, working 6 mm ($\frac{1}{4}$ in) in from the edges to form the ruffling.

5 Push the casing over the metal arm, letting it gather up to fit (fig **2**). Tighten the open end with a few hand stitches so that the casing doesn't slip off the arm during use.

SMOCKED TIEBACK

The smocking has been achieved by using ready-made heading tape. Tieback depth will be determined by the depth of the heading tape you buy. You will need twice the tieback length in fabric to gather the tape (see Headings, *page 94*).

You will need
Fabric
Smocked heading tape
Two small curtain rings to hook each tieback to the wall

Measuring and cutting out
1 Read through the measuring up notes at the beginning of the Tiebacks section. Decide on the length and width of your tieback. For each tieback cut one piece of fabric to twice the desired length plus 3 cm ($1\frac{1}{4}$ in) by the width of the heading tape plus 10 cm (4 in).

2 Cut one piece of heading tape to the ungathered length of the tieback plus an allowance for turnings (*see page 96*).

Making up
3 Fold over 1.5 cm ($\frac{5}{8}$ in) to the wrong side at the ends of the tieback piece and press. Fold over 3.5 cm ($1\frac{3}{8}$ in) to the wrong side along the long edges and press.

4 Attach the tape to the wrong side of the fabric following the manufacturer's instructions. Position it so that the turned-under ends line up with the ends of the tieback and there is a 1.5 cm ($\frac{5}{8}$ in) margin of fabric along the sides.

5 Draw up the loose cords at the unknotted end of the tape until the tieback is the right length. Knot the cords but do not cut off.

6 Attach a ring centrally to each end of the tieback just to the wrong side.

BOW TIEBACK WITH CONTRAST LINING AND EDGING

This tieback is a simple length of fabric tied in a bow around the curtain. The contrast lining is cut larger than the top fabric so that it forms an edging.

You will need
Fabric
Contrast lining
A small ring to hook each tieback to the wall
Length of string or cord at least 2 metres/yards long

Measuring and cutting out
1 Read through the measuring up notes at the beginning of the Tiebacks section. Instead of a tape measure use a length of string or cord tied in a bow round the curtain to ascertain how long your bow length should be. Decide how wide it should be inclusive of the contrast edging.

2 For each tieback cut or make up one strip of top fabric measuring the finished length plus 2 cm ($\frac{3}{4}$ in) by the finished width. Cut or make up the same number of contrast lining strips, each measuring the tieback length plus 2 cm ($\frac{3}{4}$ in) by the width plus 4 cm ($1\frac{1}{2}$ in).

3 With the right side of the top fabric strip facing, mark a point on the long side edge 3 cm ($1\frac{1}{4}$ in) from the bottom right-hand corner. Repeat at the other end, measuring from the bottom left-hand corner. Cut from the top corner to these points and you will have equally angled ends (fig **3**). Repeat the process to match on the lining strip.

Making up
4 With right sides together, match the raw edges of one long side of the fabric and lining strip. Baste along this side, then stitch, taking a 1 cm ($\frac{3}{8}$ in) seam allowance. Stitch the strips together along the other long side. The lining strip will curl up slightly.

5 Turn the bow length the right side out and press so that the lining forms a 1 cm ($\frac{3}{8}$ in) margin of fabric down either side (fig **4a**) of the tieback.

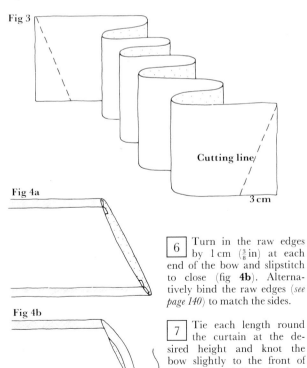

Fig 3

Cutting line

3 cm

Fig 4a

Fig 4b

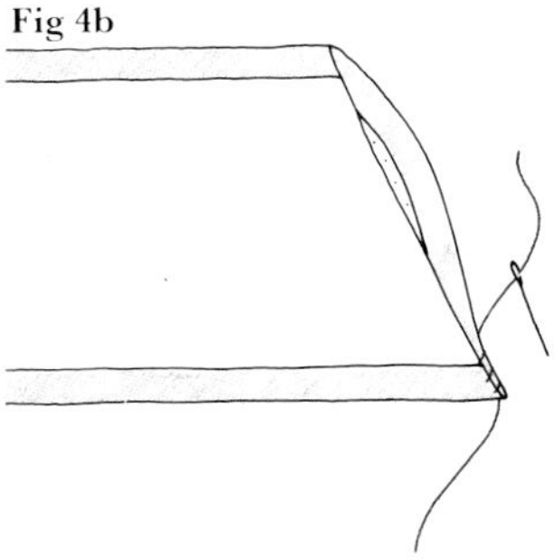

6 Turn in the raw edges by 1 cm ($\frac{3}{8}$ in) at each end of the bow and slipstitch to close (fig **4b**). Alternatively bind the raw edges (*see page 140*) to match the sides.

7 Tie each length round the curtain at the desired height and knot the bow slightly to the front of the curtain. Adjust the bow as necessary so that it is evenly tied. Make a small mark on the bow length where it should be attached to the hook at the side of the curtain. Undo the bow and attach a curtain ring to the right side of the bow length at the marked position. Place the ring over the hook and re-tie the bow round the curtain.

LINED TIEBACK WITH CORD AND CONTRAST EDGING

This tieback is threaded with decorative twisted cord which is drawn up around the curtain. The lining is cut larger than the fabric and forms a contrast edging all round. Specific measurements have been given for this tieback, but you may wish to adapt these to suit your curtains.

You will need
Fabric
Contrast lining
Length of silky twisted cord about 2 metres/yards long for each tieback
Two small curtain rings to hook each tieback to the wall

Measuring and cutting out
1 For each tieback cut one fabric strip 47 cm ($18\frac{1}{2}$ in) long by 15 cm (6 in) wide and one contrast lining strip 53 cm (21 in) by 21 cm ($8\frac{1}{2}$ in) wide.

Making up
2 With raw edges even, right sides together and the lining overlapping each end of the fabric by 3 cm ($1\frac{1}{4}$ in), stitch the fabric and lining together along each long edge, taking a 1.5 cm ($\frac{5}{8}$ in) seam allowance. The lining will curl up slightly.

3 Turn the tube right side out and press so that a 1.5 cm ($\frac{5}{8}$ in) contrast edging is formed on the front side (fig 5). Trim the seam allowances to 6 mm ($\frac{1}{4}$ in) if necessary.

4 At each end of the tube turn under the excess lining twice, folding over the fabric to form the edging (fig 6). Slipstitch (*see page 140*) in place.

5 Mark the centre of the tieback along its length. The first buttonhole position should be marked across this line 2.5 cm (1 in) from one end, the second 6 cm ($2\frac{1}{2}$ in) from the first buttonhole and

Fig 5

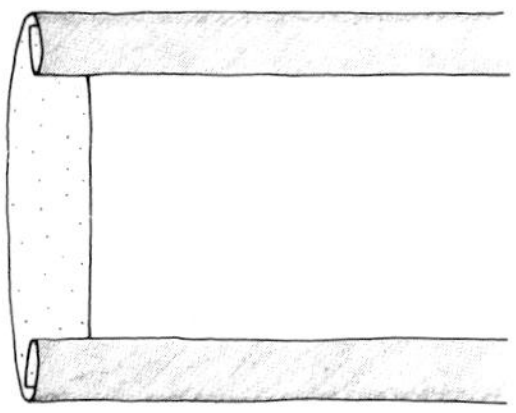

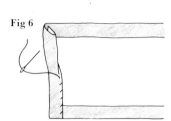

Fig 6

Fig 7

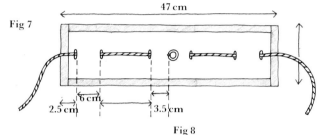

47 cm

6 cm

2.5 cm   3.5 cm

the third 11.5 cm ($4\frac{1}{2}$ in) from the second buttonhole (fig **7**). Repeat from the other end.

[6] Make 1.5 cm ($\frac{5}{8}$ in) buttonholes at each marked point either by machine or hand (*see page 139*) through both the fabric and contrast lining.

[7] Attach the ring to the centre of each tieback as indicated. Thread the cord through the buttonholes, beginning on the right side of the tieback. Place round the curtain. Draw up and adjust to fit.

STIFFENED TIEBACK WITH CONTRAST EDGING AND ROSETTE

The lining of this tieback is wider than the top fabric and forms a contrast edging along the sides.

You will need
Fabric
Contrast lining
**Pelmet (cornice) buckram or
    similar stiffening**
**Two small curtain rings to hook
    each tieback to the wall**
**Cotton wool (batting) for
    stuffing the rosette button**

Measuring and cutting out the tieback

[1] Read through the measuring up notes at the beginning of the Tiebacks section. Decide on the finished length and width of your tieback inclusive of edging.

[2] For each tieback cut one piece of top fabric measuring the finished length plus 2 cm ($\frac{3}{4}$ in) by the finished width. Cut one piece of contrast lining measuring the tieback length plus 2 cm ($\frac{3}{4}$ in) by the width plus 4 cm ($1\frac{1}{2}$ in). Finally cut one piece of buck-

Fig 8

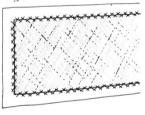

Fig 9

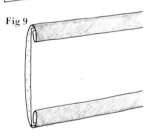

30 cm

Cutting line

Fig 10

Fig 11

Fig 12

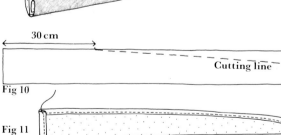

ram to the finished length and width measurement minus 1 cm ($\frac{3}{8}$ in) all round.

Making up

[3] Lay the buckram centrally over the wrong side of the top fabric piece, the seam allowance forming a 1 cm ($\frac{3}{8}$ in) margin around the buckram. Baste together. Herringbone stitch (*see page 139*) the edges of the buckram to catch it to the fabric. The horizontal stitches should be placed just within the fabric seam allowance (fig **8**) so they won't show on the right side when the fabric is folded over.

[4] With right sides together and raw edges even, stitch the tieback front to the lining along the long edges, taking a 1 cm ($\frac{3}{8}$ in) seam allowance and leaving one end open. Be careful to sew close to but not over the edge of the buckram.

[5] Turn to the right side and press, smoothing the seam allowances towards the outer edge of the tieback. The lining will form a 1 cm ($\frac{3}{8}$ in) margin along each side (fig **9**).

[6] At the open ends of the tieback turn 1 cm ($\frac{3}{8}$ in) to the inside and slipstitch (*see page 140*) the folded edges together to close.

[7] Hand stitch a curtain ring to the centre of each tieback end just on the wrong side.

Cutting out the rosette

[8] First make up the pattern. Draw a rectangle 100 cm ($39\frac{1}{2}$ in) long by 11.5 cm ($4\frac{1}{2}$ in) wide. At one end mark a point halfway down its width. Mark another point on the long edge about 30 cm (12 in) from the top corner of the opposite end. Beginning at the bottom right hand corner, join the marks, curving the line up to the halfway point (fig **10**). Cut out the pattern.

[9] Using the pattern cut out the rosette strip from the main fabric. Cut a circle of contrast fabric 6 cm ($2\frac{1}{2}$ in) in diameter.

[10] Turn in the strip curved side and end twice to the wrong side by 6 mm ($\frac{1}{4}$ in) each time, and stitch (fig **11**). Press.

[11] Make two rows of gathering stitches 1 cm ($\frac{3}{8}$ in) and 1.5 cm ($\frac{5}{8}$ in) from the remaining raw edge. Gather the strip until it looks suitably ruffled. Secure the threads at each end by winding them in a figure of eight round a pin.

[12] Beginning at the narrow end of the strip, start winding it round and round and carefully build up the rosette (fig **12**), adjusting the gathers as necessary and pinning firmly as you work. Position the neatened end so that it won't show. Secure the rosette with a few hand stitches through its centre.

[13] To make the contrasting centre, run a line of gathering stitches around the outer edge of the circle and gather up, stuffing a small wad of cotton wool (batting) into the centre as you do so, to form a soft ball (fig **13**). Secure the gathering threads by knotting them around the neck of the ball. Stitch to the centre of the rosette, tucking any raw edges out of sight.

[14] Attach the completed rosette to the outside of the tieback, positioning it roughly 5 cm (2 in) from the outer end.

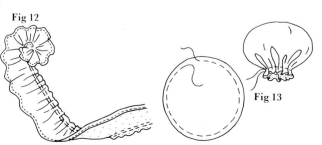

Fig 13

SHAPED INTERLINED TIEBACK WITH OPTIONAL PIPING AND ROSETTE

Besides being stiffened and lined, this curved tieback has an interlining. The lining is attached by hand. The tieback is deepest at the middle and tapers gradually to the ends.

You will need
Fabric
Curtain lining sateen
Domette or bump (flannel or flannelette) for the interlining
Pelmet (cornice) buckram or similar stiffening
Pre-shrunk piping cord (if making piping)
Two small curtain rings for hooking each tieback to the wall
Pattern or graph paper
Contrast fabric and 2 cm ($\frac{3}{4}$ in) self-cover button for the optional rosette

Measuring and cutting out

1 Read the measuring up notes at the beginning of the Tiebacks section. Decide on the length and depth of your tieback. Next take a rectangle of pattern/graph paper the proposed length of the tieback by a width of at least 30 cm (12 in), and fold in half. Mark the tieback depth, A-B, on the foldline. Using the folded edge as the centre of the tieback draw the curved shape freehand (fig **14**). Cut out the pattern and hold it against the curtain to see if the proportions are right. Adjust or cut another pattern if necessary.

Half tieback length

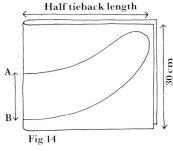

Fig 14

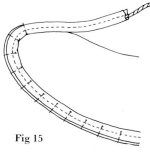

Fig 15

2 For each tieback cut one piece of interlining and one piece of buckram using the pattern. Next, adding a 1.5 cm ($\frac{5}{8}$ in) seam allowance all round, cut out one piece of fabric and one of lining.

3 If you are attaching piping, cut out enough bias strips (*see page 140*) to cover the required length of piping cord when joined.

Making up

4 Lay the interlining centrally over the wrong side of the fabric so the fabric seam allowance forms an even margin around the edge. Lay the buckram over the interlining and pin in place. Herringbone stitch (*see page 139*) the buckram and interlining to the fabric as described in step 3 of the previous tieback instructions, making sure that the stitches don't go through to the front when you stitch through the buckram and interlining.

5 *For piping only.* Make up enough covered piping (*see page 141*) to go all the way round the edges of the tieback. With raw edges matching and with the piping against the right side of the top fabric (fig **15**), stitch the piping to the fabric, using the zipper foot on the machine and joining the piping (*see page 141*) at the end of a tieback.

6 Fold the fabric seam allowance (and that of the piping if applicable) over the buckram and pin. Cut notches in the inward curves to take out excess fabric. Press. Set aside.

7 Turn the lining edges to the wrong side by 1.5 cm ($\frac{5}{8}$ in) and press, cutting notches to take out the excess fabric as before. Set the lining over the wrong side of the tieback and slipstitch (*see page 140*) in place all round the edge (fig **16**).

8 Press the completed tieback and attach a ring centrally at either end just on the lining side.

Optional rosette

9 Cut one strip of contrast fabric 69 cm (27 in) long by 10 cm (4 in) wide, and one strip of self fabric 56 cm (22 in) long by 7.5 cm

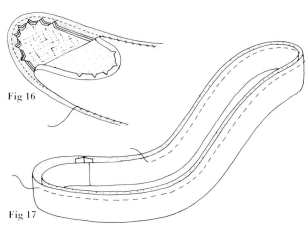

Fig 16

Fig 17

(3 in) wide. Cover the self-cover button with the contrast fabric.

10 Fold the contrast strip in half widthways and stitch the raw ends together to make a circle, taking a 1 cm ($\frac{3}{8}$ in) seam allowance.

11 Fold the circle in half lengthways, wrong sides together and matching raw edges. Stitch the raw edges together, taking a 6 mm ($\frac{1}{4}$ in) seam allowance (fig **17**). Press.

12 Make large gathering stitches around the circle 6 mm ($\frac{1}{4}$ in) from the raw edges. Draw up to a tight centre, gathers forming even folds. Secure gathering stitches.

13 Repeat steps 10 to 12 for the self fabric, set this gathered circle on top of the larger circle, matching centres. Stitch together at the centre.

14 Attach the button to the centre of the rosette. Stitch the rosette to the tieback.

BLINDS

ROMAN BLIND

Roman blinds give a tailored uncluttered finish to a window, lying flat when lowered but pulling up to form neat horizontal pleats. Made from closely woven fabric and lined, they are fixed at the top of the window to a length of wooden battening. Fine cords run up through lengths of ringed tape stitched to the back of the blind and are threaded through screw eyes driven in on the underside of the batten, which channel the cords to one side of the blind. The excess cords are then wound round a cleat fixed at the side of the window recess when the blind is raised. A wooden lath is slotted through the blind at the base to weight the edge (fig **1**).

The rings on the tapes at the back of the blind are

lined up horizontally, and these form the pleats when the cords are pulled up. A distance of 10 cm (4 in) between the rows of rings would give 5 cm (2 in) deep pleats, which would be suitable for small windows. On larger windows allow between 15 and 20 cm (6 to 8 in) between rows for 7.5 cm (3 in) to 10 cm (4 in) pleats. The flap at the bottom of the blind should be half the distance between the rows of rings.

When hanging against a recessed window the blind will fit against the recess ceiling. When hanging outside a recess or against a non-recessed window, the batten will have to be positioned above the recess/window frame at the desired height. You can paint the batten or cover it with fabric to match the blind.

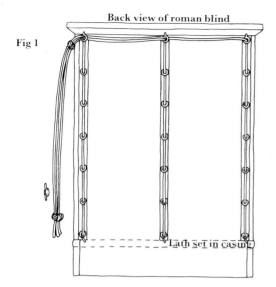

Fig 1

Back view of roman blind

Lath set in casing

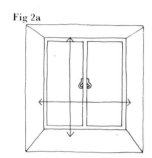

Fig 2a

Fig 2b

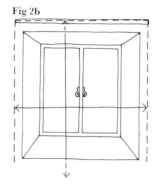

Fig 2c

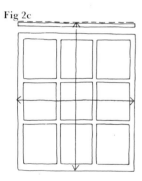

You will need

Fabric
Lining
Length of 50 mm by 25 mm
  (2 in by 1 in) wooden battening
  the finished width of the blind
Narrow pocketed tape
Split rings
Nylon cord
Lath, 25 mm by 5 mm (1 in by
  $\frac{1}{4}$ **in)**
Metal angle brackets plus
  screws (for the battening)
Cleat

Measuring and cutting out

1 Measure for the *finished* width and length of the blind. *Blind set in a recess:* Measure the width and height

of the recess (fig **2a**). *Blind set outside a recess:* Measure the width and height of the recess and extend the blind by at least 5 cm (2 in) either side. To the height measurement add whatever overlap you require at the top and bottom of the window (fig **2b**). *Blind set against a non-recessed window:* Measure the width and height from frame outer edge to outer edge. To the height add whatever overlap you require at the top of the window (fig **2c**).

2 *Top fabric.* To calculate the amount of fabric needed for each blind add 6 cm (2$\frac{1}{2}$ in) to the finished length measurement for the top turning and seam allowance, and add 6 cm (2$\frac{1}{2}$ in) to the width. *Lining.* Add 6 cm (2$\frac{1}{2}$ in) to the finished length measurement only; the width of the lining is the same as the finished width of the blind.

3 Cut out one piece of top fabric and one piece of lining to these dimensions for each blind.

Making up

4 Mark the centres of both fabric pieces at the top and bottom with tailor's chalk on the wrong side. Set the lining against the fabric with right sides together and raw edges even and pin, baste and stitch down the sides. Turn the right side out.

5 Pin the fabric pieces together at the marked centres at the top and bottom of the blind and, lined side upwards, press the side seams. The top fabric will form a 1.5 cm ($\frac{5}{8}$ in) margin down the sides of the blind.

6 Turn inside out again and stitch across the bottom of the blind, taking a 1.5 cm ($\frac{5}{8}$ in) seam allowance. Turn to the right side and press.

7 Lay the blind out flat with the lined side uppermost and mark the position of the lath casing by measuring up from the blind base to a distance equal to the depth of the bottom flap (see introduction above). Draw a straight line across the blind at this point and then draw a second line,

Fig 3

Lath casing

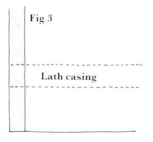

Fig 4

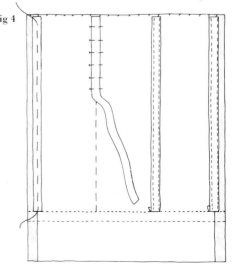

parallel to the first, 4 cm (1$\frac{1}{2}$ in) above. Stitch along these marked lines to form the lath casing. You can unpick the stitching at one seamline at a later stage to insert the lath. (fig **3**).

8 Mark vertical lines for the tapes on the wrong side of the blind with chalk or pins. These should be placed at equal distances apart about every 30 cm (12 in) with the first and last rows positioned over the side seamlines by about 12 mm ($\frac{1}{2}$ in) in. They should run from the lath casing to the top of the blind.

9 Cut one length of tape to the correct length, allowing for 1 cm ($\frac{3}{8}$ in) turn-under at one end. Measure off the rest against it, making sure the pockets are aligned. Position the tapes over the marked lines, turning under the raw ends at the lath casing (fig **4**). Baste down the tape centres to hold and then stitch down each side.

10 Insert split rings in each tape at equal distances apart up the blind, beginning just above the lath casing and checking that they line up horizontally (fig **1**).

11 Unstitch one of the seamlines at the side of the casing. Cut the lath to the finished curtain width minus 1 cm ($\frac{3}{8}$ in). Insert the lath and slipstitch (*see page 140*) the seam to close.

12 Measure up the finished length of the blind

from the base and mark across the top. Zigzag the fabric and lining together along the top edges to neaten. Lining up the marked line with the top edge of the battening, wrap the blind over the top of the battening and tack or staple in place. Make sure you attach the blind so it hangs straight.

13 Position a screw eye in the underside of the battening to correspond with the rows of tape. Screw brackets to the underside of the board where they are going to butt up against the window/wall.

14 Cut the cord into as many lengths as there are rows of tape. Each length should measure twice the length of the finished blind plus one width.

15 Tie a cord to each bottom ring and thread it up through the rings on the tape. Pass each cord through a screw eye and then towards the side from which you wish to operate the blind, taking the cord through each screw eye it passes (fig **1**). Continue until all the cords are hanging together at the side of the blind, threaded through one screw eye. Knot together about 2.5 cm (1 in) outside screw eye. Do not cut cords.

16 Fix the battening in position. Then attach a cleat to the side of the recess, wall or window edge. Knot the cords level with the window base. Pull up the blind and wind the ends around the cleat to anchor.

Fig 5

AUSTRIAN BLINDS

These blinds work on the same principle as the Roman blind. However, they have a gathered or pencil pleated heading and need a fullness of two to two and a quarter times the batten length. They look like curtains when let down and form scallop shapes along the base edge when raised. If made slightly longer than the window and pulled up fractionally, the base edge will form scallops even when the blind completely covers the window. Austrian blinds can be lined, but beware of them looking unwieldy when drawn up. Fewer scallops drape better if making a heavier blind.

To produce the bound ruffled edge on page 8, place a standard gathered heading tape the desired depth down from the blind top, attach the tape without folding the top over, and bind the top edge. The single ruffle has also been bound.

UNLINED AUSTRIAN BLIND WITH DOUBLE RUFFLE

You will need
Fabric
Pencil pleat heading tape
Curtain hooks
Narrow pocketed tape (see Roman blind)
Thin nylon cord
Split rings
Large screw eyes for underneath of batten
Smaller screw eyes to take curtain hooks, set in the front edge of batten
Length of 50 mm by 25 mm (2 in by 1 in) battening
Cleat

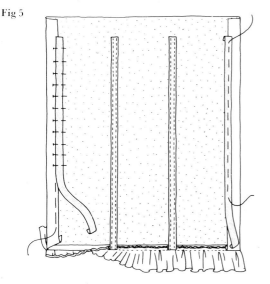

Measuring and cutting out

1 See Roman blind, step 1, for instructions on measuring the window. To the length add 3.5 cm (1⅜ in) for the base hem and heading allowance. Calculate the width of the blind as explained on page 95 of Curtains, allowing 3 cm (1¼ in) on each side for hems. Join widths if necessary to make up a fullness of two to two and a quarter times the batten length (adding too much fullness will make the swags droopy) and match any pattern across seams (*see page 139*). Join widths with French seams if they are not to be covered with lengths of tape (*see page 140*).

2 Cut strips of fabric that measure twice the depth of the ruffle (7.5 cm/3 in) plus 3 cm (1¼ in) seam allowance by a length that equals the finished width of the blind when the strips are joined up. Allow 1.5 cm (⅝ in) for seams on each strip end.

3 Make up the ruffle complete with gathering stitches, breaking the gathering at intervals along the ruffle edge if necessary (*see page 142*). Do not pull up the gathering yet. Turn in the raw ends at each side by 1.5 cm (⅝ in) and slipstitch (*see page 140*) to close. Press.

4 At the base edge of the blind place pins 3 cm (1¼ in) from each side edge. Divide up the base edge between these pins into the same number of sections as the ruffle edge. With raw edges even position the ruffle against the right side of the blind between the outer pins, so that the side hem allowances are left free. Matching the pins along the ruffle and blind edges, draw up the ruffle to fit. Stitch the ruffle

Fig 6

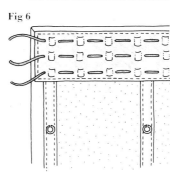

to the blind, taking a 1.5 cm (⅝ in) seam allowance. Zigzag stitch or oversew (*see page 140*) the two allowances together to neaten the edges and press upwards.

5 Press the side seams to the wrong side and baste in place.

6 Decide how many scallops you would like across the finished blind. Divide the batten length into equally sized scallops and add one to give the number of vertical rows of tape needed. For example, four scallops will need five rows of tape. The tapes are positioned at equal distances across the ungathered blind; the distance between them will be two to two and a quarter times the finished scallop width, depending on the fullness you allowed. They should run from the ruffle seamline to within 6 cm (2½ in) of the blind top, allowing for 1 cm (⅜ in) turn-under at the ruffle end.

7 Position the two outer rows of tape over the raw edges of the side hems (fig **5**) and place the remaining lengths at equal distances in between (see step 9, Roman blind).

8 Press 2 cm (¾ in) to the wrong side at the top of the blind. Apply heading tape (*see page 110, step 9*) 3 mm (⅛ in) down from the top edge (fig **6**).

9 Insert split rings in each tape about 20 cm (8 in) apart, beginning 3 cm (1¼ in) from the ruffle seam and ending about 15 cm (6 in) from the blind top. Make sure the levels of the rings match horizontally. Cut and attach the cords as for the Roman blind, step 15.

10 Draw up the heading tape to fit the batten. Insert a curtain hook at each end of the blind and then at 6 cm (2½ in) intervals in between.

11 Attach the large screw eyes to the underside of the batten to correspond with the rows of tape. Attach screw eyes along the front of the batten to correspond with the curtain hooks (fig **7**).

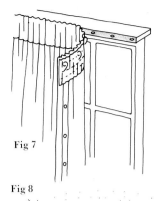

Fig 7

Fig 8

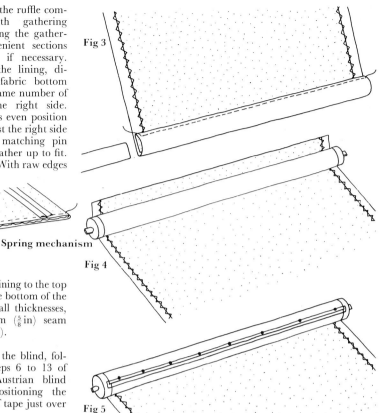

Fig 3

Spring mechanism

Fig 4

Fig 5

3 Make up the ruffle complete with gathering stitches, breaking the gathering into convenient sections (*see page 142*) if necessary. Pulling back the lining, divide the top fabric bottom edge into the same number of sections on the right side. With raw edges even position the ruffle against the right side of the fabric, matching pin markers, and gather up to fit. Baste in place. With raw edges even stitch the lining to the top fabric across the bottom of the blind through all thicknesses, taking a 1.5 cm ($\frac{5}{8}$ in) seam allowance (fig **8**).

4 Complete the blind, following steps 6 to 13 of the unlined Austrian blind instructions, positioning the outer lengths of tape just over the side seams.

ROLLER BLIND

The fabric on the roller blinds shown in this book rolls over the front of the roller rather than from the back, because it is printed. If it rolled from the back you would see the unprinted side showing on the roller. The angled attic window blind on page 92 can be set at various heights because the lath at the bottom of the blind extends beyond the edges to slot into grooves cut into the window frame.

12 Fix the batten in position and attach the blind by slotting a curtain hook through each of the screw eyes on the front. Thread the cords through the large screw eyes underneath as for the Roman blind, step 15.

13 Fix the cleat in position and pull the cords to raise the blind. Knot at sill level and wind the excess around the cleat.

LINED AUSTRIAN BLIND WITH RUFFLE

Besides the items needed for the unlined Austrian blind above, you will also require lining cut to the dimensions given in step 1 below.

Measuring and cutting out

1 Measure for the top fabric as described in step 1 above. Cut the fabric to the same length but allow 4.5 cm ($1\frac{3}{4}$ in) on each side for seams. Cut a piece of lining that measures the same length as this top piece, but 3 cm ($1\frac{1}{4}$ in) narrower than the blind's finished width.

Making up

2 Mark the centres of the lining as for the Roman blind, step 4. Stitch together down the sides, taking a 1.5 cm ($\frac{5}{8}$ in) seam allowance. Turn to the right side and pin the centres together. With the lined side uppermost, press the blind so that a 3 cm ($1\frac{1}{4}$ in) margin of top fabric is formed down the sides. Turn back to the wrong side again.

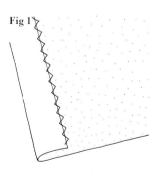

Fig 1

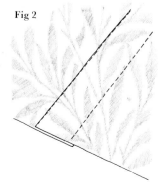

Fig 2

You will need

A roller blind kit (see step 1). These usually include a **wooden roller with a spring fitted at one end, two brackets a wooden lath for the bottom of the blind, tacks, cord and acorn, and a cord holder.**
Mediumweight fabric
Fabric stiffener (optional)
Set or L-square (optional)

Preparing the roller and fabric

1 Decide whether you are going to hang your blind inside or outside the window recess—blinds are usually hung inside the recess. Measure the width of the recess. If you are hanging the blind outside the recess allow extra for overlap (*see page 110*).

Roller blind kits come in standard widths. Unless the blind width you need is a standard size, buy the next size up and cut the roller and lath to fit.

2 Usually two different brackets are supplied with each kit. One takes the spring end of the blind, which should go on the right if you are using a printed non-reversible fabric. Fix the brackets in place in the recess, allowing for the pin end and spring mechanism at each end of the roller. Allow a gap of 3 cm ($1\frac{1}{4}$ in) at the top to take the full roller. Measure the distance between the brackets and saw the roller to this width if necessary, making an allowance for the end cap which you still have to fit. Fit the end cap, following the kit maker's instructions.

3 If you want to stiffen your fabric this should be done before cutting to size, following the instructions provided with the stiffener.

Measuring and cutting out

4 Measure the width of the roller excluding the pin ends and deduct a further 12 mm ($\frac{1}{2}$ in) to obtain the finished blind width. Add 2 cm ($\frac{3}{4}$ in) to the width if you are not using stiffened fabric. Allow for the centring of any design you wish to feature and for extra fabric if your blind is very wide, and patterns have to be matched across seams when lengths are joined (*see page 139*).

5 Using an expandable metal ruler, measure the drop of the blind from the top of the brackets down to the sill adding 30 cm (12 in) for the bottom casing thus ensuring that the roller is still covered when the blind is fully extended.

6 Working on a flat surface, cut the fabric to size, using a set or L-square and metre/yard stick, making sure the corners are square and the ends straight (otherwise your blind will hang crooked). Use a sharp cutting knife or scalpel and a steel ruler as a guide if you are cutting stiffened fabric.

Making up

7 *Unstiffened fabric.* At each side edge turn in the edges for 1 cm ($\frac{3}{8}$ in). Pin, baste and zigzag stitch the edges in place, positioning the zigzag stitches centrally over the raw edges (fig **1**). If working with a machine that won't zigzag, work two rows of straight stitching close together down each edge. *Stiffened fabric.* There should be no need to turn in the side edges as the fabric should be fray resistant. Zigzag stitch the side edges if the fabric shows any tendency to fray. *Joining fabric widths.* Match patterns across seams (*see page 139*) overlapping the fabric in the usual way if using unstiffened fabric. There is no need to turn under a seam

allowance if joining stiffened fabric. Overlap the fabric widths so the patterns match and topstitch down both long edges to secure (fig **2**).

8 At the base turn under 4 cm (1$\frac{1}{2}$ in) twice to make a double hem (turn the hem over once only if using stiffened fabric). Stitch across the hem close to the folded inner edge and across one end to make a casing for the lath. Trim the lath to fit the casing minus 12 mm ($\frac{1}{2}$ in). Insert the lath and stitch across the open end of the casing (fig **3**).

9 Next make up the cord pull. Thread one end of the cord through the holder and knot, then thread the opposite end through the acorn. Screw the cord holder centrally to the lath on the right side of the blind. (You can screw it to the back if you wish to hide the holder.)

10 Lay the blind fabric flat *wrong* side upwards. Lay the roller on the fabric at the top with the spring mechanism to the *left* (fig **4**). Lift the edge of the fabric over on to the roller lining it up with one of the horizontal guidelines on it. Stick the edge of the fabric temporarily in place with tape and hammer tacks through the fabric into the roller at 2 cm ($\frac{3}{4}$ in) intervals, with one at each end (fig **5**).

11 Roll the fabric up tightly around the roller and fit it in the brackets. Pull the blind down to its full extent. When you give a gentle tug the blind should roll up correctly. If it doesn't do so, or the tension is sluggish remove the extended blind from the brackets and rewind by hand. Put the blind back in the brackets, extend again and give it a tug to make it roll up. The blind should now be at the correct tension.

LOOSE COVERS

SCROLL-ARMED SOFA WITH PIPING AND KICK-PLEATED SKIRT

The sofa on page 10 has been covered in striped fabric. If you close one eye and squint, the strongest stripe—the red one—will leap forward. When using boldly patterned fabric, you should feature the part that is the most eyecatching. For example, position a prominent motif at the centre of a piece of furniture and work outwards, as has been done with the red stripe on the sofa cover. Large floral motifs should be centred on cushions; each scroll should be a mirror image of the other. Stripes should match across the inside and outside arm joins and run down the chair back, seat, front and skirt in continuous matching lines as on page 10.

You may find that you have to join widths of fabric to make up the seat front, inside and outside back. In this case, centre one full width of fabric and attach narrow panels at either side. Patterned fabric should be carefully matched across seams (*see page 139*).

The sofa skirt has six inverted pleats, one at each corner, centre back and front. The opening of the cover is placed at the back right-hand corner (looking at the sofa from the back) and begins

just below the scroll. The sofa on page 10 has a fixed cover, but a snugly fitting loose cover can be achieved by securing the bottom edges of the cover under the sofa. This is done by tightening a cord threaded through a casing, which can be released when you wish to remove the cover.

Measuring the sofa

1 Remove any cushions and draw a diagram of your sofa from the back and front as shown (figs **1** and **2**). Make a list of the sections to be covered and label each one. Then measure each section lengthways and widthways at the widest point, making length measurements to the floor as indicated in figs **1** and **2**.

2 Write down these measurements against your list and indicate on the drawing which way the lengthways grain should run (as a general rule towards the floor).

3 Add 15 cm (6 in) tuck-in allowance to the lower edge of the inside back (A), inside arm (C) and to the sides and back of the seat (B). Add a tie-under allowance of 15 cm (6 in) minus the distance I–J (fig **1**) to the lower edge of the outside back (G), and the seat front (F). To the outside arms (D), add this allowance (15 cm/ 6 in minus I–J) plus the width measurement of the arm front (E) across the base. Add 5 cm

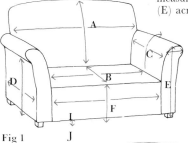

Fig 1

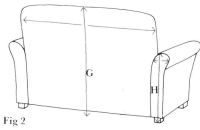

Fig 2

(2 in) to all the remaining edges for pin-fitting adjustment, with the exception of the hem edges on the arm fronts and backs.

4 Decide on the finished depth of the skirt. In these instructions 15 cm (6 in) has been allowed, but it may be that a different depth would look best on your sofa. If you are unsure, cut a piece of stiff card to the proposed depth and prop it up in front of the sofa. Stand well back and see if the proportions look right (fig **3**). Having made any adjustments, the same piece of card can be used with tailor's chalk to mark a line around the bottom of the chair so the skirt can be positioned accurately (see step 29).

5 To calculate the overall width of the skirt, measure round the outside of the chair at the bottom and add 20 cm (8 in) for each pleat, plus a further 10 cm (4 in) for adjustment/seam allowances at each end of the skirt. Add 5 cm (2 in) to the skirt depth for seam allowance and hem.

If you are using fabric with a pattern that has to be matched vertically as on page 10 or one which would show up seamlines, calculate fabric widths so seams are hidden in the pleats.

6 Measure the cushions in the same way as for rectangular box edged cushion with zip and piping (*see page 119*). If the cushions have a down filling and can be pushed through a narrow opening, there is no need to extend the zip around the corners of each cover, and it can be positioned along one of the back edges. This means you require only one piece of fabric for the back gusset (boxing strip), the same length and width as the front.

Estimating the fabric

7 Draw the pattern pieces on graph paper to the correct scale following your measurements. Label the pieces and mark the direction of the lengthways grain. You will have to allow roughly 5/6 fabric widths to make up the skirt. Don't forget to add on seam allowances of 1.5 cm ($\frac{5}{8}$ in) for the joins. Cut out the pieces.

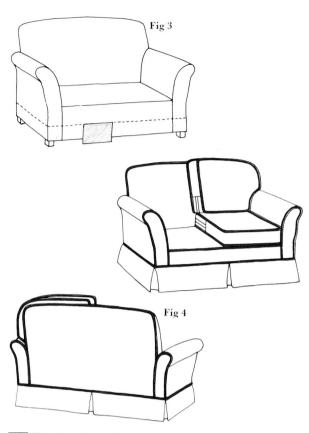

Fig 3

Fig 4

8 Keeping the scale the same, draw a long rectangle to the width of your chosen fabric. For plain fabric arrange the pieces as closely as possible, keeping the grain line of the pieces parallel with the graph paper 'selvedges'. If you are using patterned fabric mark in the length of the pattern repeat or where the main design motifs fall, and position the pieces accordingly.

9 Measure the length of the plan and convert it to full scale to find out the amount of fabric you need. Use waste areas of fabric for the piping strips or add extra to the total amount (*see page 113* for fabric estimate). Fig **4** indicates where the piping should run. Allow extra piping for joins and tucking into seams (about 38 cm/15 in).

You will need
Fabric
Contrasting fabric (optional) for piping bias strips (*see page 141*). (Make sure it is the same type as the main fabric because a different weight material could cause puckering when the cover is washed or dry cleaned.)

Pre-shrunk piping cord
Zips (zippers) for the cushions
Large hooks and eyes
Piece of strong cord long enough to go round the widest part of the sofa with plenty over for tying
Sharp pair of scissors
Upholstery pins and skewers (T-pins)
Tailor's chalk
Metre/yard stick
Expandable metal ruler
Stiff piece of card 13.5 cm ($5\frac{3}{8}$ in) by 30 cm (12 in)

Making up

10 Lay the fabric out smoothly, having ironed out any deep creases. Using a set or L-square and ruler, mark out all the basic rectangles in tailor's chalk according to your plan. Follow the lengthways grain carefully, keeping sides straight and corners square. As you cut out, label each piece on the wrong side with chalk and indicate which end is the top.

11 Next mark down the centre of all the sofa sections with tailor's chalk (fig **5**). Repeat, to mark a central line down the wrong side of the corresponding fabric sections.

12 Start by pinning the outside back in position. Place the fabric rectangle *right side out* out over the sofa back, matching centres. Smoothing the fabric out from the centre, secure in position with pins or upholstery skewers (T-pins) pushed in along the top edge of the sofa (fig **6**). (All fabric pieces should be placed on sofa right side out and pinned with wrong sides together.)

13 Repeat this sequence with the inside front, placing the tuck-in allowance at the base. Pin the outside and inside back sections together at the top and sides, making small pleats if necessary at curved corners to take in fullness (fig **7**). Make sure that you push the pins well home so they do not spring out when the cover is lifted off, and avoid catching them in the chair fabric, or the cover will be difficult to remove. Chalk in the seamline and remove the skewers (T-pins) and/or pins from the sofa. Trim round the seam as neatly as possible, leaving an even seam allowance of about 2 cm ($\frac{3}{4}$ in).

14 Set the inside arm in place, positioning the tuck-in allowance at the base. Pin to the inside back including to the tuck-in allowance, which should be folded over the seat. If necessary, allow for tuck-in at the inside arm corners, between the arm and the sofa back (fig **8**).

15 Position the outside arm and pin it to the inside arm just underneath the scroll. Trim seams to 2 cm ($\frac{3}{4}$ in) and chalk in seam allowances.

16 Next position the arm fronts. Hold the material in place with upholstery skewers (T-pins). If you are using patterned fabric, move the sections around until the two arms are matching. Pin each piece to the inside and outside arms, taking the seams to the floor. This pinning should be as tight and accurate as possible. Trim the seams to 2 cm ($\frac{3}{4}$ in) and clip curves to ease.

17 Position the arm backs in the same way. Mark

the top of the back opening 7.5 cm (3 in) below the inside/outside arm join.

18 Matching the centres, smooth the seat piece in position, tuck-ins to the sides and back.

19 Pin the tuck-in allowances together at the inside back and sides of the sofa, taking a 1.5 cm ($\frac{5}{8}$ in) seam allowance (fig **9**). Fit the tuck-in carefully at the back corners and front side edges. You may find you don't need much tuck-in here as some sofa seats are fixed at these positions. You will then have to taper the tuck-in to fit.

20 Position the seat front piece against the sofa and pin to the seat piece and arm front. If the sofa isn't fixed at the front edges pin the seat front piece to the tuck-in allowance as well as the arm front and seat (fig **10**).

21 Check all the seamlines are chalked in, and the cover fits evenly and snugly. Then trim all the excess fabric at the seams to 1.5 cm ($\frac{5}{8}$ in). Take out the pins/skewers (T-pins) you have used for positioning the cover pieces. Remove the cover carefully from the sofa, taking out only as many pins from the seams as necessary.

22 If you haven't yet done so, make up the covered piping (*see page 141*). The piped seams on the cover are indicated in fig **4**, but you can pipe any seam that outlines the sofa.

23 Removing a few pins from the cover at a time, reverse all the seams (so that the right sides of the fabric are together), repinning and inserting the piping where appropriate as you go along. Leave the back opening unpinned and the piping dangling. It will be attached when you make a facing for the opening. The back piping begins at the skirt edge, goes across the sofa back, and down to skirt height again. Begin the arm back piping in the outside back/arm back seamline. To avoid bulky seams pull back the covering from the piping end for 1.5 cm ($\frac{5}{8}$ in) and cut away the cord. The flat covering is then stitched into the seam.

24 Baste the cover together firmly. Turn to the right side and check that the seams reveal an even amount of piping.

25 Stitch all the seams that do not have piping.

Then change to a zipper foot on the machine and stitch round the fronts and backs of both arms, and then round the sofa back.

26 Next make up the tie-under flaps (fig **11**). Starting with the right front corner (looking at the sofa from the front), measure how far back the leg extends (fig **12a**). Then measure from the top of the arm front to the sofa base edge and add 1 cm ($\frac{3}{8}$ in) (fig **12b**). Mark this depth in tailor's chalk across the base of the *cover* arm front and then along the outside arm up to where the leg extends (point Y). Using a set or L-square or a large book, line up point Y with the outside arm tie-under edge and mark point Z 5 cm (2 in) further along. Rule a diagonal line in tailor's chalk from point Y to point Z. At the right-hand corner of the seat front tie-under flap measure 5 cm (2 in) to the left (point W). Rule a diagonal line from point W to point X on the arm front/seat front seam. Cut along the chalked line from W to Z. Turn under

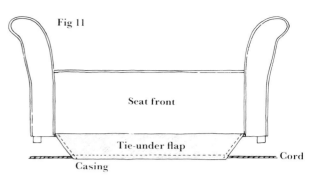

Fig 11

Seat front

Tie-under flap

Casing

Cord

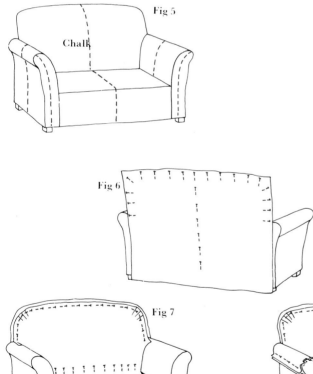

Fig 5

Chalk

Fig 6

Fig 7

Fig 8

Inside back

Inside arm

Tuck-in allowances

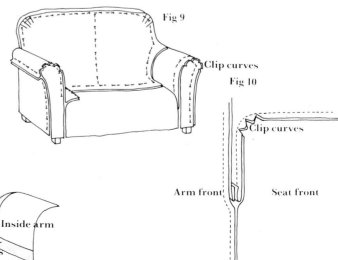

Fig 9

Clip curves

Fig 10

Clip curves

Arm front

Seat front

the cut edge by 1 cm ($\frac{3}{8}$ in) and stitch. Repeat at each corner to produce angled flaps and hemmed arm fronts and backs.

27 Turn under top edge of each flap by 12 mm ($\frac{1}{2}$ in) then 2.5 cm (1 in) and stitch close to hem edge to make a casing for the cord (fig **12c**). Make another row of stitches just above previous row to strengthen.

28 Thread cord through the casing and fit the cover over the sofa. Pull the flaps under the sofa, but don't tighten the cord as you will have to remove the cover to attach the skirt. (Don't cut off excess cord when you do finally tighten it; tuck ends under one of the flaps.)

29 Using the card, mark skirt line around the sofa with chalk (fig **2**). It should be skirt depth minus 1.5 cm ($\frac{5}{8}$ in) from the floor.

30 Join the strips to make up the complete skirt width. Turn under 1 cm ($\frac{3}{8}$ in) and then 2.5 cm (1 in) along the base edge. Hem in place by hand or machine. Press.

31 To form the pleats, start at the opening edge, lining up the end of the skirt, right side out, with the raw edge of the opening and matching the skirt seamline

against the line chalked on the sofa. The skirt edge will be lower than the base edge of the opening. Fold half an inverted pleat at the corner (fig **13a**). Pin the skirt along sofa back. At each corner form an inverted pleat (fig **13b**). At the last corner, the opening edge, fold back half a pleat as before. Cut back any excess fabric to the opening edge seam allowance.

32 Remove the skirt from the cover, being careful to keep the pleats pinned in place. Baste across the top of each pleat to hold and press.

33 Raw edges even, baste and stitch piping to the skirt on right side (fig **14**).

34 With right sides together and skirt upside down, pin the skirt to the cover along stitching line of the piping; raw edges should line up with the chalk line marked round the cover (fig **15**).

35 Remove the cover from the sofa and baste and stitch the skirt in place, using the zipper foot, to enclose the piping in the seam. Oversew raw edges and press.

36 To face the back opening, cut a strip of self-fabric the length of the opening plus 2 cm ($\frac{3}{4}$ in) by 13 cm ($5\frac{1}{4}$ in) wide. Turn under 1 cm

($\frac{3}{8}$ in) at one end and stitch across the hem. Fold in half lengthways with wrong sides together and press. Press under 1.5 cm ($\frac{5}{8}$ in) along the long raw edges of the strip and encase the seam allowance of the outside arm and the skirt (fig **16**), placing the strip 1 cm ($\frac{3}{8}$ in) above the top of the opening. Stitch along seamline, leaving the top 1 cm ($\frac{3}{8}$ in) unattached.

37 Cut another strip the length of the opening plus 2 cm ($\frac{3}{4}$ in) by 7.5 cm (3 in) wide. Hem the bottom edge as before. Press and machine under 1 cm ($\frac{3}{8}$ in) down one long edge.

38 With raw edges even, baste the loose piping to the right side of the arm back piece and the skirt along the opening, bending back the cord into the seam allowance at the bottom and cutting it away as explained in step 23.

39 Right sides together and raw edges even, stitch the strip to the opening, leaving 1 cm ($\frac{3}{8}$ in) excess at the top.

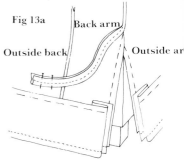

Fig 13a

Back arm

Outside back

Outside ar

Fig 13b

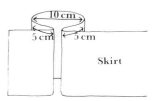

10 cm

5 cm   5 cm

Skirt

Turn the strip to the inside of the opening (fig **17**). Press.

40 Hand sew the two strips together and finish off the raw edges. Attach the hooks to the piped section of the opening and eyes to the other (fig **18**).

41 Make up the cushion covers (*see page 119*).

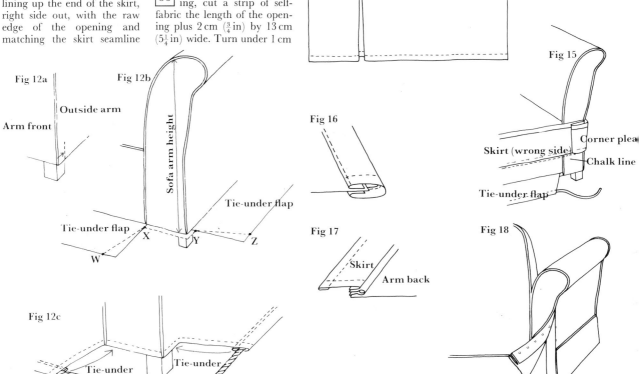

Fig 12a

Fig 12b

Outside arm

Arm front

Sofa arm height

Tie-under flap

Tie-under flap

X   Y   Z

W

Fig 12c

Tie-under   Tie-under

Fig 14

Fig 15

Fig 16

Corner plea

Skirt (wrong side)

Chalk line

Tie-under flap

Fig 17

Skirt

Arm back

Fig 18

CUSHIONS

Cushions are the simplest way of providing finishing touches to sofas, beds, and chairs. They add comfort and colour and can be made in any shape or size. They can even be used as seating units.

The cushions in this section have been set out in their basic forms to which 'extras' can be added, such as covered piping, single or double ruffles, ruffles with contrast edgings. There are many different ways to close a cushion cover; slipstitching is the easiest. Alternatives are zips (zippers), Velcro, press fasteners (snaps), ties, buttons with holes and loops. The cushion cover is sewn to fit over a cushion pad. You should never put loose fillings straight into a cushion cover. The cushion pad can either be bought or made up if you want an unusual shape or size. Make sure the fabric used for the pad cover is compatible with the filling. Feather fillings require a covering of feather-proof cambric. (See page 120 for cushion pad instructions.) For a plump cushion, leave out the cushion cover seam allowances. Bold symmetrical patterns on fabric should be suitably placed on the cushion. A large floral design is usually centred for example. If you find it difficult to calculate how much patterned fabric you will need to make your cushion(s), make a pattern to the correct size and position it over the fabric before buying, to ascertain exactly how much you need.

KNIFE-EDGED CUSHION COVERS

These can have a side or back opening. The back opening in these instructions is closed with a zip (zipper), but other methods can be used according to preference. The side opening in the following types of cover is either zipped or slipstitched closed. Slipstitching is the simplest and most unobtrusive way of closing a cover, but the opening will have to be restitched every time the cover is cleaned and the seam won't withstand a great deal of strain.

Fig 1

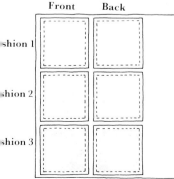

SQUARE OR RECTANGULAR CUSHION COVER WITH SIDE OPENING

You will need
Cushion pad

Fabric, including an allowance for ruffles (*see page 142*) and/or piping (*see page 141*) if required

Zip (zipper) (optional) the same size as the cushion opening (see step 9)

Pattern paper or metre/yard stick and tailor's chalk

Fabric tape measure

Fig 2

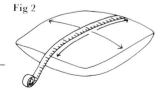

Measuring and cutting out

1 Using the fabric tape measure, measure the pad from seam to seam across its centre in both directions (fig **1**). Add 1.5 cm ($\frac{5}{8}$ in) seam allowance all round.

2 For each cushion you will need two pieces of fabric cut to the required size. If you are making several cushions, calculate how many cover pieces will fit into the fabric width and draw a cutting plan (fig **2**). To estimate the amount of fabric needed add up the measurements of the marked pieces down the length. For example, to make three 38 cm (15 in) square cushions you would need 82 cm ($32\frac{1}{2}$ in) of 137 cm (54 in) wide fabric.

3 Next make a paper pattern for each cover piece if desired.

4 Lay the fabric out flat and position the pattern pieces or, using the metre/yard stick as a guide, mark out the cover squares or rectangles in tailor's chalk following the straight grain of the fabric.

Making up

5 *Hand-sewn side opening.* Cut two pieces of fabric for each cushion, allowing 1.5 cm ($\frac{5}{8}$ in) for seams all round.

6 Attach ruffles and/or piping at this stage. *For a single or double ruffle* work gathering stitches along half the ruffle length and then cut the gathering threads. Make gathering stitches along the remaining length. With raw edges even and the right side of the ruffle against the right side of one of the main cover pieces, gently pull the gathering threads along half the ruffle length until this exactly fits two sides of the cover. Fit the remaining half of the ruffle in the same way. Baste ruffle in place 1 cm ($\frac{3}{8}$ in) from the cover edge (fig **3**). Clip corner.

After it has been made up a *pleated ruffle* should be basted to a cover piece with raw edges even, right sides together. *Piping* should be attached in the same way. If it is to be used with a ruffle, it should be applied first and the ruffle basted in place on top (fig **4**). Corners should be clipped to ease.

7 Place the fabric pieces with right sides together and stitch round three sides. On the unstitched side sew in 5 cm (2 in) from both ends, leaving the centre of the seam open. Trim down the seam allowance to 1 cm ($\frac{3}{8}$ in), cutting across the corners (fig **5**). Neaten the raw edges with machine zigzagging or oversew by hand. Turn the cover to the right side and press carefully, making sure the corners are fully pulled through by using a pin, very gently, to ease them out.

8 Insert the cushion pad. Turn in the opening edges in line with the remainder of the seam and slipstitch (*see page 140*) to close.

9 *Zip (zipper) fastened side opening.* Follow steps 5 and 6 above. With the opening edges of the two cushion pieces even and right sides together, stitch in for 5 cm (2 in) from each end of the seam. Baste along the rest of the seam; this forms the opening. Press the seam open. Set in the zip (zipper) (*see page 141*) and open it. Follow the instructions for

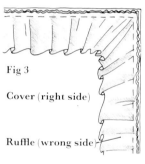

Fig 3

Cover (right side)

Ruffle (wrong side)

Fig 4

Cover (right side)

Piping

Fig 5

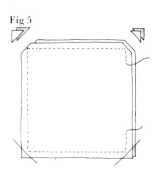

Fig 6a

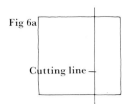

Cutting line

Fig 6b

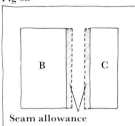

B   C

Seam allowance

Fig 6c

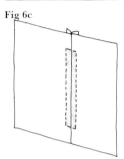

inserting a zip (zipper) in a piped seam if you have applied piping.

10. With right sides together, stitch round the remaining unstitched edges of the cover and finish as in step 7. Insert the cushion pad.

SQUARE OR RECTANGULAR CUSHION WITH BACK ZIP (ZIPPER) OPENING

If the cover fabric is very thick and difficult to work, a zip set in the back of the cushion is easier to sew.

You will need
Cushion pad
Fabric, including an allowance for a ruffle (*see page 142*) and/or piping (*see page 141*) if desired
Zip (zipper), the length of the widest side of the cushion less 10 cm (4 in)
Pattern paper

Measuring and cutting out

1. Calculate how much fabric you will need, following steps 1 and 2 of the square or rectangular cover with side opening.

2. Cut out two pattern pieces to equal the cushion pad measurements (fig 1) plus

seam allowances of 1.5 cm ($\frac{5}{8}$ in) all round.

3. Set one pattern piece, marked A, aside, then draw a line across the other piece 6 cm ($2\frac{1}{2}$ in) in from one side. Cut along this line (fig **6a**). Mark pieces B and C.

4. Lay all the pattern pieces on the fabric following the straight grain, adding a 1.5 cm ($\frac{5}{8}$ in) seam allowance to the newly cut edges of B and C (fig **6b**). Cut out.

Making up

5. With right sides together and raw edges even, stitch B and C together for 5 cm (2 in) in from each end. Baste the remainder of the seam. Press the seam open and insert the zip (zipper) (*see page 141*) (fig **6c**).

Fig 7

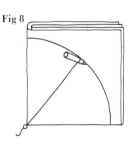

Front   Back

Cushion 1

Cushion 2

Cushion 3

Cushion 4

Fig 8

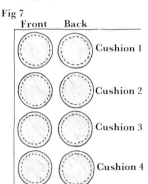

Fig 9

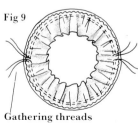

Gathering threads

Fig 10

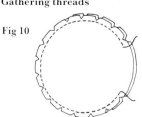

6. Attach ruffle and/or piping to the cover top at this stage if desired (see step 6 for square or rectangular cover with side opening).

7. Open the zip (zipper). With right sides together and raw edges even, stitch the cover pieces together. Finish as for square or rectangular cushion with side opening, step 7. Turn to the right side. Insert the cushion pad.

ROUND CUSHION COVER WITH HAND-SEWN SIDE OPENING

You will need
Cushion pad
Fabric, to include an allowance for ruffles (*see page 142*) and/or piping (*see page 141*) if desired
Pattern paper
Length of string and pencil
Fabric tape measure

Measuring and cutting out

1. Using a fabric tape measure, measure the diameter of your cushion pad and add 3 cm ($1\frac{1}{4}$ in) for seam allowances. This gives the diameter of each cover piece. If you are making several covers, work out how many pieces will fit into the fabric width and draw a cutting plan (fig **7**). Add up the measurements of the cover pieces down the length of the fabric to find the amount you require. For example, to make covers for four 30 cm (12 in) diameter cushions you would need 66 cm (26 in) of 137 cm (54 in) wide fabric.

2. Take a square of pattern paper slightly larger than the cover diameter. Fold it into quarters. Attach a length of string to the lower end of a pencil and cut this off to equal half the diameter of the cover. (For a plump cushion subtract 1.5 cm/$\frac{5}{8}$ in seam allowance.)

3. Lay the paper on a board and pin the loose end of string to the point of the folded corner with a thumb tack or drawing pin. Draw an arc from one side of the folded paper to the other. Cut along the marked line and unfold your pattern (fig **8**).

4. Using the pattern, cut two cover circles from

the fabric.

Making up

5. Make up the optional ruffle and/or piping. *For a single or double ruffle work gathering stitches along half the ruffle length and then cut the gathering threads. Make gathering stitches along the remaining ruffle length. Fold one of the cover circles in half and mark the halfway point at the raw edges. Open out again. With raw edges even and the right side of the ruffle against the right side of the cover, position each break in the gathering at the marked points. Gently pull the gathering threads so that the ruffle fits evenly round the cover. Baste the ruffle in place 1 cm ($\frac{3}{8}$ in) from the cover edge (fig **9**).*

After it has been made up a pleated ruffle should be basted to a cover piece with raw edges even, right sides together. Piping should be attached in the same way. If it is to be used with a ruffle, it should be applied first and the ruffle basted in place on top.

6. With right sides together and raw edges even, stitch round the circles, leaving a gap of roughly one third of the circumference through which to turn. Trim the seam allowance to 1 cm ($\frac{3}{8}$ in) if the fabric is bulky, then notch all round the seam allowance (except for the opening) to ease (fig **10**).

7. Turn the cover to the right side and add the cushion pad. Turn in the opening edges in line with the remainder of the seam and slipstitch (*see page 140*) to close.

ROUND CUSHION COVER WITH BACK ZIP (ZIPPER) OPENING

You will need
Cushion pad
Fabric, to include an allowance for ruffle (*see page 142*) and/or piping (*see page 141*) if desired
Zip (zipper), the length of the line drawn one third of the way down your cushion (*see step 2*) less 10 cm (4 in)
Pattern paper
Length of string and pencil

Measuring and cutting out

[1] Measure and cut out the pattern pieces as in steps 1 to 4 above. Set one piece aside, marked A.

[2] Taking the other pattern piece, draw a line across it roughly one third down (fig **11**). Cut along this line and mark the pieces B and C.

[3] Cut out all the cover pieces, adding a 1.5 cm ($\frac{5}{8}$ in) seam allowance to the newly cut edges of the B and C pieces (see fig **12**). Remember to feature any large pattern on the front of the cover.

[4] With raw edges even and the right sides of B and C together stitch along the seam for 5 cm (2 in) in from each end (fig **13**). Baste the remainder of the seam and set in the zip (zipper) (*see page 141*) (fig **14**).

Fig 11
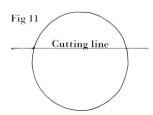
Cutting line

Fig 12
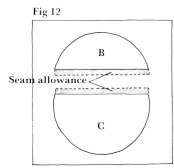
B
Seam allowance
C

Fig 13
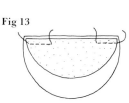

Fig 14
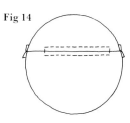

[5] Make up and attach optional ruffle and / or piping, following step 5 for the round cushion cover with hand-sewn side opening.

[6] Open the zip (zipper). Continue as for the round cover with hand-sewn side opening, steps 6 and 7, omitting the side opening.

HEART-SHAPED COVER WITH DOUBLE RUFFLE AND PIPING

You will need

Fabric and filling to make up a cushion pad (*see page 117*)
Cover, ruffle and piping fabric
Zip (zipper) (*see step 5*)
Pre-shrunk piping cord
Pattern paper

Cutting out the pattern

[1] Cut a rectangle of pattern paper slightly larger than your intended cushion pad, say 38 cm (15 in) across by 35 cm (14 in) down. Fold the paper in half lengthways and draw half a heart, taking the fold as the central point and using a plate or bowl to help draw the curve if necessary. Cut round the shape while still folded in half, then open out. Mark this pattern piece A (fig **15**).

[2] Draw round A on another piece of pattern paper and cut out duplicate piece B.

[3] Take pattern piece B and rule a straight line across it at its widest point (fig **16**). Cut along the line, to make two pattern pieces.

[4] Cut out the cover front using pattern A. Cut the back pieces using the two pattern B sections, adding a seam allowance of 1.5 cm ($\frac{5}{8}$ in) to the newly cut back opening edges (see fig **17**).

Making up

[5] With right sides of the B sections together and raw edges even, stitch 5 cm (2 in) in from each end along the back opening seam. Baste the remainder of the seam to close. Press the seam open and set in the zip (zipper) (*see page 141*).

[6] Cut out enough bias strips (*see page 140*) to cover the required length of

Fig 15
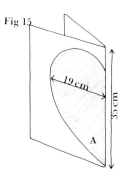
19 cm
35 cm
A

Fig 16

Cutting line

Fig 17
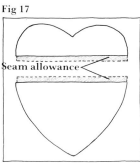
Seam allowance

piping cord (see step 8) when joined.

[7] For the ruffle cut a strip of fabric 13 cm ($5\frac{1}{4}$ in) wide by twice the length of the outer edge measurement of the heart.

[8] Make up the cushion pad as explained on page 120, taking a 1.5 cm ($\frac{5}{8}$ in) seam allowance. Make up enough covered piping to go round the heart plus 3 cm ($1\frac{1}{4}$ in) seam allowance. Make up the ruffle as explained on page 142, dividing the gathering stitches into two sections.

[9] With raw edges even, baste the piping to the heart front, joining the ends (*see page 141*) wherever seems most unobtrusive.

[10] Now attach the ruffle. With raw edges even, position the breaks in the gathering threads at the point of the heart and the dip and pull up each ruffle section so that it gathers evenly around the heart. Baste 1 cm ($\frac{3}{8}$ in) from heart edge.

[11] Open the zip (zipper). Continue as for the round cushion cover with hand-sewn opening, steps 6 and 7, omitting the side opening.

BOX EDGED CUSHION COVERS

Adding a gusset (boxing strip) to a cushion cover produces a deeper three-dimensional shape, which gives a more tailored finish to the cushion and allows for a more solid filling. The gusset (boxing strip) itself is the strip of fabric that is inserted between the top and bottom pieces of the cover. It can be pleated, made in a contrasting or decorative fabric. Piping can be inserted in seams between the gusset (boxing strip) and top and bottom pieces.

The cushion covers that follow have a zip (zipper) set in the gusset (boxing strip). If you are making more than one cushion it may be helpful to draw up a cutting plan as in fig **2** page 117 (square and rectangular covers) and fig **7** page 118 (round cushions), allowing for the gusset (boxing) strips. Read through the introduction to Cushions for other basic information.

SQUARE OR RECTANGULAR BOX EDGED COVER WITH PIPING

If you are making a cover for an inflexible cushion pad, such as a thick piece of foam or a sprung cushion, the zip should extend around the cover corners. This means the back gusset (boxing strip) will extend round the corners as well (fig **18a**). If the cushion pad is flexible the zip (zipper) can be set into a back-width gusset (boxing strip) (fig **18b**).

You will need

Cushion pad
Zip (zipper) 10 cm (4 in) shorter or 10 cm (4 in) longer than the cushion back (see above)
Fabric
Contrast fabric (optional) for piping bias strips (*see page 140*)
Pre-shrunk piping cord
Pattern paper (optional)

Measuring for the cover

[1] For the top and bottom piece of the cushion cover measure the top and bottom surfaces of the pad in

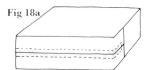

Fig 18a

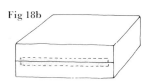

Fig 18b

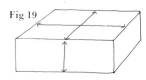

Fig 19

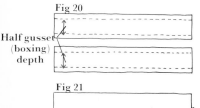

Fig 20

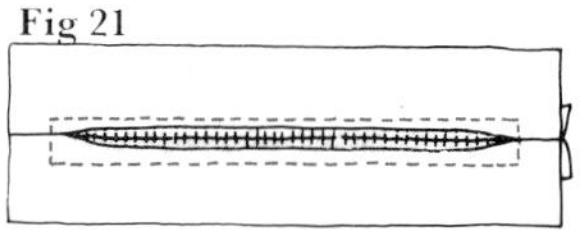

Half gusset (boxing) depth

Fig 21

both directions and add 1.5 cm ($\frac{5}{8}$ in) for seam allowances all round (fig **19**).

2 For the gusset (boxing) pieces, measure the length and depth of the sides and front of the pad and add 1.5 cm ($\frac{5}{8}$ in) seam allowance all round. Measure the length of the back gusset (boxing strip) and add 3 cm ($1\frac{1}{4}$ in) for seams. As this strip will be cut in half lengthways so the zip (zipper) can be inserted, add 6 cm ($2\frac{1}{2}$ in) to the depth of this piece (fig **20**).

For a cover with a rigid filling measure the length and depth of the cushion back and add 18.5 cm ($7\frac{1}{4}$ in) to the length and 6 cm ($2\frac{1}{2}$ in) to the depth for the zip (zipper) and side seam allowances. Measure the length and width of the cushion sides and subtract 7.5 cm (3 in) from the length. Add 1.5 cm ($\frac{5}{8}$ in) seam allowance all round. Measure the length and width of the cushion at the front and add 1.5 cm ($\frac{5}{8}$ in) for the seam allowance all the way round.

3 Cut out pattern pieces to these measurements if desired.

4 Cut out enough bias strips (*see page 140*) to cover sufficient piping to go round the cushion twice plus an allowance for joins.

5 Lay the fabric out flat and position the pattern pieces or, using the metre/yard stick as a guide, mark out the cover squares or rectangles in tailor's chalk following the straight grain of the fabric. For each cushion cover, cut out one top piece, one bottom piece and four gusset (boxing) pieces—one front, one back and two sides.

Making up

6 Cut the back gusset (boxing strip) in half lengthways. Place the two halves right sides together. On an ordinary back-width gusset (boxing strip), stitch in from each end for 2 cm (2 in) along the seam allowance. Baste along the remainder of the seam. Press open and insert the zip (zipper) (*see page 141*). If the gusset (boxing strip) is to extend round the cushion corners stitch in from each end for 4 cm ($1\frac{1}{2}$ in) along the seam allowance and repeat the process just described (fig **21**).

7 Right sides together, raw edges even, stitch gusset (boxing) strips together into a ring. Press seams open.

8 Make up enough covered piping (*see page 141*) to go round each cushion twice, allowing for joins.

9 Beginning at the back of each cushion, with raw edges even, pin piping around the cushion top and then the bottom, joining the ends neatly (*see page 141*). Clip the corners to ease

10 Matching seams to corners and with right sides facing, stitch the gusset (boxing strip) to one of the main cover pieces, using the zipper foot on the machine. Trim diagonally across the seam allowances at the corners to reduce bulk. Open the zip (zipper) and then attach the remaining main piece in the same way.

11 Press the seam allowances towards gusset (boxing strip), trimming to 1 cm ($\frac{3}{8}$ in). Insert cushion pad.

ROUND BOX EDGED CUSHION WITH PIPING

You will need
Fabric
Cushion pad
Zip (zipper) (*see step 2*)
Contrasting fabric for piping bias strips
Pre-shrunk piping cord

Measuring for the cover

1 Measure the diameter of the cushion pad and add 3 cm ($1\frac{1}{4}$ in). This gives the diameter of the top and bottom of the cushion cover.

2 Measure the depth and the circumference of the

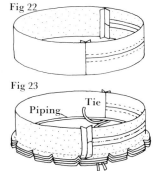

Fig 22

Fig 23

Piping   Tie

pad. Cut one gusset (boxing) piece to measure half the circumference plus 3 cm ($1\frac{1}{4}$ in) by the depth plus 3 cm ($1\frac{1}{4}$ in). Cut a second strip for the zipped section to measure half the circumference plus 3 cm ($1\frac{1}{4}$ in) by the depth plus 6 cm ($2\frac{1}{2}$ in). The zip (zipper) should measure about 4 cm ($1\frac{1}{2}$ in) less than half the cushion circumference. If you won't be able to squash the cushion pad through this opening, make the zipped section of the gusset (boxing strip) longer and adjust the front section to fit.

3 Cut sufficient contrast bias strips (*see page 140*) to cover enough piping to go round the cushion twice plus an allowance for joins.

Making up

4 Insert the zip (zipper) in the back gusset (boxing) strip (*see page 141*).

5 Join the strips into a ring. Press seams (fig **22**).

6 Make up the piping and attach to the right side of the top and bottom cover pieces, raw edges even.

7 Attach the gusset (boxing strip) to the main cover pieces as in steps 10 and 11 of the previous instructions. Clip into the seam allowances all the way round the cover to ease the fabric (fig **23**). Press all seams towards the gusset (boxing strip). Turn the cover to the right side and insert the pad.

SHAPING CUSHIONS TO FIT THE CHAIR SEAT

Many wooden or cane chairs have an irregularly shaped seat, sometimes with jutting struts or arms. The cushion pad can be cut from foam or made up to fit (*see page 120*). To shape it accurately you need to make a paper pattern of the seat.

Cutting out the pattern

1 Measure the width and depth of the chair seat and cut a piece of paper slightly larger. Lay the paper on the chair and pencil around the edges to make an exact outline of the seat.

2 If you are making a cushion for a sofa or armchair back remember that it will sit on top of a seat cushion, so lay your pattern piece over the sofa/chair back with the seat cushion(s) in place.

3 The pattern pieces can now be used to make the cushion pads and to cut out the cushion cover. For box edged cushions with curved sections cut to fit round the arms of a chair, insert the zip (zipper) into the widest part of the bottom piece of the chair cover so it won't show (see square or rectangular cushion cover with back fastening).

MAKING A CUSHION PAD

You will need
Foam chips, feathers or feathers and down, according to preference and type of cushion being made
Ticking (for foam chips)
Down-proof cambric (for feathers)
Strong thread
Pattern paper

Making up

1 Cut a pattern in the intended shape and size of your cushion.

2 Cut out the fabric pieces required, adding a 1.5 cm ($\frac{5}{8}$ in) seam allowance all round, and omitting openings for back and gusset (boxing strip) zips (zippers) and trimmings.

3 Make up the cushion pad case in the same way you would the cushion cover, leaving a gap in one seam through which to stuff the case. Stitch around the case twice, one row just above the other, for strength.

4 Clip across corners diagonally and clip curves. Turn to the right side.

5 Fill the case firmly. Slipstitch (*see page 140*) the opening edges together in line with the remainder of the seam to close.

ATTACHING THE CUSHION TO THE CHAIR WITH TIES

When placed on upright wooden or cane chairs, such as those found in dining rooms and kitchens, cushions need to be firmly attached and the simplest solution is to tie them to the chair back struts.

You will need
Two pieces of fabric 61 cm (24 in) by 5 cm (2 in) to match or contrast with the cushion cover

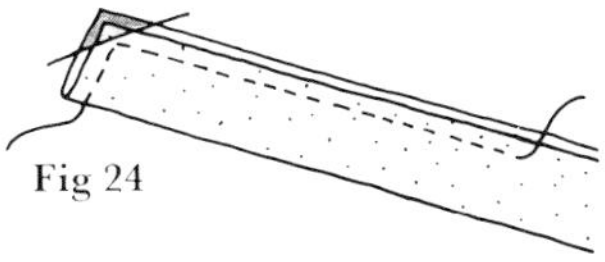

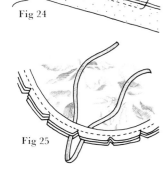
Fig 24

Fig 25

Fig 26

Making up
1 Fold each strip in half lengthways, right sides together and matching raw edges. Stitch across one end and along the length of each tie 1 cm ($\frac{3}{8}$ in) from the raw edge. Trim the stitched corner (fig **24**) and turn the ties right side out, using the blunt end of a pencil to facilitate turning. Press the ties. Turn in the raw edges at the un-stitched ends and slipstitch (*see page 140*) to close.

Attaching the ties to knife-edged covers
2 Before you have sewn the cover pieces together but after attaching any ruffle and/or piping, set one of the cover pieces on the chair and mark on the seam allowance the positions of the two (outer) struts.

3 Fold each tie in half and place at a strut position on the right side of the cover with the folded edge even with the cover back edge (fig **25**). Baste to hold.

4 Complete the cushion cover as explained in the individual instructions.

Attaching ties to a box edged cover
5 Make up the cover as explained in the individual instructions.

6 Fold the ties in half and position them so that they align with the two (outer) struts when the completed cushion is on the chair. Stitch in place (fig **26**).

BUTTONED LOUNGER CUSHION

The lounger is backed with towelling and can be filled with foam or polyester wadding (batting). It measures 60 cm (24 in) wide by 190 cm (74$\frac{3}{4}$ in) long and is divided into a back cushion section of 68 cm (26$\frac{3}{4}$ in) and a seating section of 122 cm (48 in). To

avoid fabric wastage, you could either make two loungers from 137 cm (54 in) fabric or use the remainder of the fabric width to make matching cushions. Alternatively you may wish to make up a lounger to your own size specifications. The lounger is attached to the seat at the sides with ties.

You will need
Cushion pad cut to the finished size of the lounger, using 5 cm (2 in) thick foam or two thicknesses of 8 oz polyester wadding (batting, extra loft) (see step 5 for details)
Top fabric
Towelling (terrycloth)
24 self-cover buttons 2.5 cm (1 in) in diameter
Large embroidery needle
Cotton twine

Measuring and cutting out
1 To the desired width and length of the lounger add 8 cm (3$\frac{1}{4}$ in) for depth and seam allowances. Cut one piece of top fabric and one piece of towelling (terry-cloth) to these dimensions, making sure the top and bottom ends are at right angles to the selvedge and the long edges run parallel to it. You can make a paper pattern from pieces of newspaper pinned together if necessary.

2 On the right side of each cover piece, mark across the dividing line (fig **27**) between the back and seating lengths with tailor's chalk. This will be 72 cm (28$\frac{3}{8}$ in) down from the top edge if you are using the size specifications above.

Making up
3 Set the two fabric pieces right sides together, raw edges even and stitch all round, taking a 1.5 cm ($\frac{5}{8}$ in) seam allowance and leaving an opening at the foot of the

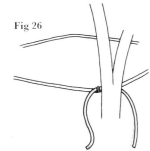
Fig 27

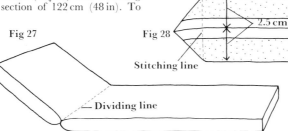
Fig 28

Stitching line

Dividing line

2.5 cm

cushion about 46 cm (18 in) wide through which to push the cushion pad.

4 To make the corners of the cover, stitch evenly across each corner through both thickness of fabric (fig **28**); the length of the stitching should measure 5 cm (2 in). Trim the corners and turn the cover to the right side.

5 Cut the cushion pad in two pieces, one to fit the back section (68 cm/26$\frac{3}{4}$ in) and the other to fit the seat (122 cm/48 in). Two layers of polyester wadding (batting) are used to obtain the correct thickness. These should be stitched together loosely with diagonal rows of basting before inserting into the cover.

6 Insert the cushion back foam or wadding (batting) into the top part of the cover and then pin and baste across the marked line, matching the marking on each side of the cover. Stitch from side to side through all thicknesses. Insert the remaining larger piece of foam into the lower part of the cover. Turn in the bottom edges in line with the remainder of the seam and slipstitch (*see page 140*) to close.

7 Cover 12 buttons with the top fabric and the other 12 with the towelling (terrycloth). Mark their positions at equal intervals on both sides of the lounger. Fig **29** gives the spacing for a 60 cm (24 in) by 190 cm (74$\frac{3}{4}$ in) lounger.

8 Thread the embroidery needle with a length of twine. Holding on to the loose end of twine, push the needle through the cover from the base to the top side at the first button position. Thread on a button and return to the base. Pull the needle clear of the fabric and thread on another button. Tie the twine ends with a slip knot (*see page 142*). Pull the twine ends until both buttons sink into the cover and tie off around the shank of the button. Trim the ends of twine and push them under the button. Repeat until all the buttons have been attached.

9 Make up the ties as shown in the previous

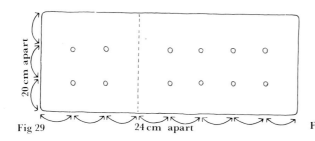

Fig 29   24 cm apart   Fig 30

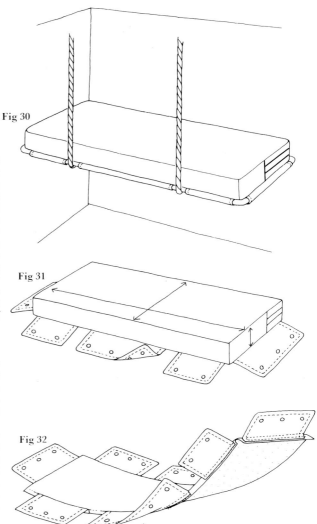

Fig 31

Fig 32

instructions, then stitch by hand to each side of the lounger at the dividing line between the back and the seat.

BUNK COVER

The rectangular box cushions in the yacht cabin on page 37 have been covered with vinyl coated fabric because it is both waterproof and strong. The seat back has a dual purpose: it sits in a frame hinged to the wall at the cushion top and can be raised at the bottom edge to make a bunk. The bunk is suspended from the ceiling by heavy ropes attached to the front of the frame which are then knotted through metal rings bolted into the ceiling. The cushion is held in the frame by means of eyeleted flaps set into the base seamline of the cushion. These flaps are lashed together with rope (fig **30**).

To make the cushion your machine will have to be capable of stitching six thicknesses of vinyl coated fabric together. You can test your machine on a small wad of fabric. If it can't stitch through all the thicknesses, hire an industrial machine for the day or take the fabric pieces to your local upholsterer to be sewn together—he can also set in the eyelets at the same time.

You will need
Fabric for the cushion
Fabric for the flaps
Velcro
Strong thread
Large eyelets
Rope

Measuring and cutting out

1 Cut out the fabric pieces needed to make up a rectangular box edged cushion (*see page 119*) with piping. The dimensions of the cushion will be determined by the size of the frame.

2 You will need to cut eight flaps, three for each side and one for each end. Fig **31** shows their relative sizes. Each flap has a finished depth of 15 cm (6 in). Allow 1.5 cm ($\frac{5}{8}$ in) all round for seams when cutting out. A gap of 7.5 cm (3 in) has been allowed for the suspending ropes and hinges. The outer side flaps and end flaps are positioned 2.5 cm (1 in) from the corners. Cut two pieces of fabric for each flap.

Making up

3 Taking a pair of flap pieces lay one over the other right sides together and raw edges even. Stitch around the three outer edges of the flap, taking a 1.5 cm ($\frac{5}{8}$ in) seam allowance, leaving the side that will be attached to the cushion unstitched. Trim corners and turn. On the right side of the flap topstitch round the three stitched sides 1 cm ($\frac{3}{8}$ in) from the edges and stitch across the open edge to close. Repeat for all the other flap pairs.

4 Apply eyelets to each flap, following the maker's instructions, placing them about 15cm (6in) apart at least 2.5 cm (1 in) in from the edges of each flap.

5 With raw edges matching set each flap in position against the right side of the cushion cover bottom piece. Stitch across the flaps twice very close together 1 cm ($\frac{3}{8}$ in) and 1.5 cm ($\frac{5}{8}$ in) in from the edges (fig **32**).

6 Follow the rectangular box edged cushion instructions to make up the cushion, double-stitching all seams for strength and inserting Velcro instead of a zip (zipper).

7 Turn the cover to the right side and place the cushion pad inside. Close the Velcro. Set the cushion in the frame and wrap the flaps around it. Thread the rope through the eyelets and crisscross the cushion base and fasten securely. The cushion is now lashed to the frame.

TABLECLOTHS

ROUND TABLECLOTHS

The following instructions are for reference, to be used when making up individual tablecloths.

Measuring and cutting out

1 First measure the diameter of the table A to B (fig **1**). Now measure to point C from the table edge for the finished drop of the cloth. Double this measurement and add it to A-B to obtain the finished diameter of the cloth. (For the vinyl coated tablecloth, sit in a chair at the table and measure the drop (B–C) to finish at thigh height.) To the finished diameter add a further 3 cm ($1\frac{1}{4}$ in) seam/hem allowance.

2 For your tablecloth you will need an amount of fabric that equals the total diameter measurement in width and length. You may find that this measurement is wider than your chosen fabric width. In this case, widths have to be joined to make up the cloth (see vinyl coated cloth, following). However, these are never joined at the tablecloth centre. Half widths are joined at the sides to

a full width of fabric positioned down the centre of the cloth. If you need to make up your cloth in this way, your fabric requirement will double in length. Remember to add a seam allowance of 1.5 cm ($\frac{5}{8}$ in) to each edge to be joined. If your tablecloth needs wider than half-width panels at each side, you will require a total fabric length of three times the cloth diameter. To match a pattern across seams add the length of one pattern repeat to the total fabric amount for each extra full width required for the side panels.

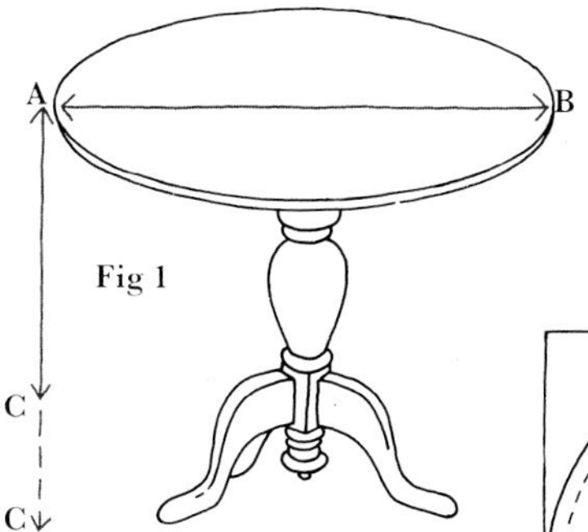

3 To make up the fabric width needed, divide the fabric into two (three if you are attaching full widths) equal lengths. For *half-width* side panels fold one section in half lengthways and cut along the fold. The remaining uncut section will form the central panel (fig **2**).

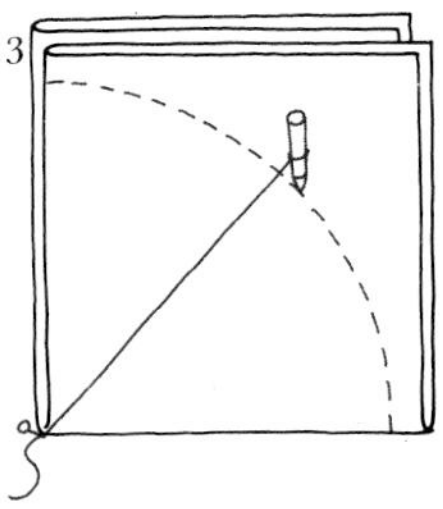

4 With right sides together and long edges even, join the tablecloth panels with flat fell seams (*see page 140*), positioning the full width of fabric in the centre. In the case of the vinyl coated tablecloth it is unnecessary to neaten the seams in this way, since the fabric does not fray or have to stand up to frequent washing. Stitch simple seams and press the allowances open, using a pressing cloth between the iron and coated fabric.

5 Fold your piece of fabric in quarters, wrong side out, and press, matching the outer edges and any seams. (Do not press folded vinyl edges.)

6 Divide the total diameter measurement arrived at in step 1 in half, to obtain the radius of the circle you are going to cut. Firmly tie a length of string longer than the radius length to the bottom of a pencil or fabric marker pen, then pin the string with a tack or drawing pin to the folded point of the fabric (fig **3**) so that the string length equals the radius when it is held taut and the pencil upright. Draw an arc across the folded fabric from edge to edge, keeping the string taut. Cut along this line through all thicknesses and open out the cloth.

ROUND VINYL COATED TABLECLOTH

As it is not a good idea to stab a drawing pin or tack through vinyl coated fabric as instructed in step 6 of *measuring and cutting out*, a paper pattern is cut for this tablecloth.

You will need
Fabric
Pattern paper
Pencil and length of string
Tailor's chalk

Making up

1 Follow steps 1 to 5 above, omitting the pressing stage in step 5.

2 To make the pattern, cut a rectangle of paper the same size as the folded cloth. Put weights on the cloth so that it lies flat and measure the edges carefully with an expandable metal rule. Mark the folded point of the fabric on the pattern.

3 Mark the pattern paper with an arc as in step 6 above. Cut along arc line.

4 Place the pattern over the fabric and weight it down, matching the folds of fabric with the pattern edges. Draw around the arc with chalk. Remove the pattern, replace the weights and cut along the arc line through the four thicknesses of fabric.

5 Unfold the cloth. Turn under 1.5 cm ($\frac{5}{8}$ in) to the wrong side all round. Stitch round 6 mm ($\frac{1}{4}$ in) from folded edge.

ROUND TABLECLOTH WITH BOUND EDGE

You will need
Fabric, following the measurements given in steps 1 and 2, but minus 3 cm ($1\frac{1}{4}$ in) seam/hem allowance added to the diameter in step 1.
Contrast bias binding (*see page 140*) 5.5 cm ($2\frac{1}{4}$ in) wide by the cloth circumference plus 5 cm (2 in)

Making up

1 Follow steps 1 to 6 of *measuring and cutting out*.

2 Make up the bias binding strip (*see page 140*). Press in 1 cm ($\frac{3}{8}$ in) to the wrong side along one long edge.

3 Set the unfolded edge of the strip against the edge of the cloth, right sides together. Fold the end of the strip 1.5 cm ($\frac{5}{8}$ in) to the wrong side (fig **4**). Pin the bias strip all round the cloth, taking a 1.5 cm ($\frac{5}{8}$ in) seam allowance. Overlap the turned-under end by about 4 cm ($1\frac{1}{2}$ in). Baste and stitch in place (fig **5**).

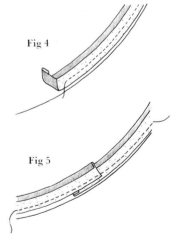

Fig 4

Fig 5

4 Clip the seam at intervals round the edge to ease.

5 Fold the bias strip over the seam allowances to the wrong side of the cloth. Slipstitch (*see page 140*) the folded edge over the previous line of stitching. Press.

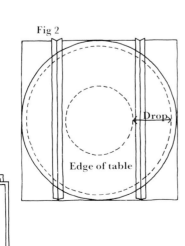

Fig 1

Fig 2

Drop

Edge of table

Fig 3

ROUND TABLECLOTH WITH BOUND AND HEADED RUFFLE

You will need

**Fabric for the main cloth and
single ruffle**

**Two contrast binding strips,
each 4 cm (1½ in) wide by the
length of the ruffle plus a
seam allowance of 3 cm (1¼ in).
These can be cut on the
straight grain, but use bias
binding (*see page 140*) if
preferred**

Making up

1 Subtracting 9 cm (3½ in) from the finished drop measurement, measure and cut out the main part of the tablecloth as described in steps 1 to 6 of measuring and cutting out at the beginning of the section (*page 123*).

2 For the ruffle, cut out enough 10 cm (4 in) wide strips to go twice round the cloth circumference when joined, allowing 1.5 cm (⅝ in) for seams at each strip end.

3 With right sides together and end edges even, join the strips into a ring with flat fell seams (*see page 140*). Press.

4 Bind both long raw edges of the ruffle exactly as for the circular tablecloth with bound edge, steps 2 to 5, taking a 1 cm (⅜ in) seam allowance. Press the bound edges.

5 Divide the ruffle into quarters, marking the dividing point of each quarter with two pins set close together. Run two lines of gathering stitches around the ruffle 1.5 cm (⅝ in) and 4 cm (1½ in) from the top bound edge, breaking the stitching lines at each set of pin markers. Set aside.

6 Turn 6 mm (¼ in) to the wrong side around the

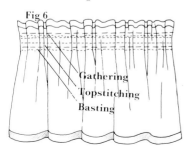

Fig 6

Gathering
Topstitching
Basting

tablecloth edge and stitch. Turn 1 cm (⅜ in) to the wrong side again and stitch close to the inner folded edge. Press.

7 Divide the edge of the tablecloth into quarters and mark with two pins as for the ruffle.

8 Matching pins, the wrong side of the ruffle against the right side of the cloth and the lower row of ruffle gathering stitches even with the cloth edge, draw up each ruffle quarter to fit the corresponding section of the tablecloth. Pin and baste in place just above or along the rows of gathering.

9 Work a row of topstitching 2 cm (¾ in) and then 3 cm (1¼ in) below the ruffle top edge (fig 6). This stitching should not overlap the gathering / basting stitches, which should now be removed.

ROUND FITTED TABLECLOTH WITH GATHERED SKIRT, PIPING AND DOUBLE RUFFLE

You will need

Fabric

Pattern paper

Tailor's chalk

Pre-shrunk piping cord

Measuring and cutting out

1 Lay a piece of pattern paper over the table top and mark round the edge in tailor's chalk. Add 1.5 cm (⅝ in) all round for seams and cut out the pattern. Use it to cut out the fabric for the table top.

2 Calculate the circumference of the table (multiply the diameter by 3.14). Double this measurement to obtain the width of the gathered skirt. Measure from the table edge to the floor or just above to obtain the drop. Subtract the desired depth of the finished ruffle from this measurement and then add 5 cm (2 in) for seams. Cut out the amount of fabric rectangles needed to make up the gathered skirt width, allowing for pattern matching across seams if necessary.

3 Cut strips of fabric to measure twice the desired depth of the ruffle plus

3 cm (1¼ in) by a finished width of twice the width of the skirt. Add 1.5 cm (⅝ in) to each strip end to allow for joins.

4 For the piping, cut enough bias strips (*see page 140*) to equal the width of the skirt when stitched together, plus an allowance for joining the ends.

Making up

5 Make up the piping (*see page 141*).

6 With right sides together and raw ends even, join the strips into a circle. Fold in half wrong sides together and top raw edges even; pin and press. Divide into sections as in step 5 of the previous instructions, running the rows of gathering stitches just above and below the seamline.

7 With right sides together and raw edges even, join the sides of the skirt rectangles together to make a circle. Attach the piping to the lower edge of the skirt, joining the ends neatly (*see page 141*).

8 Fold the skirt into four equal sections along its lower edge, marking each dividing point with two pins set close together as before. With right sides together and matching raw edges and pin markers, gather up the ruffle to fit the corresponding sections of the skirt. Stitch in place.

Fig 7

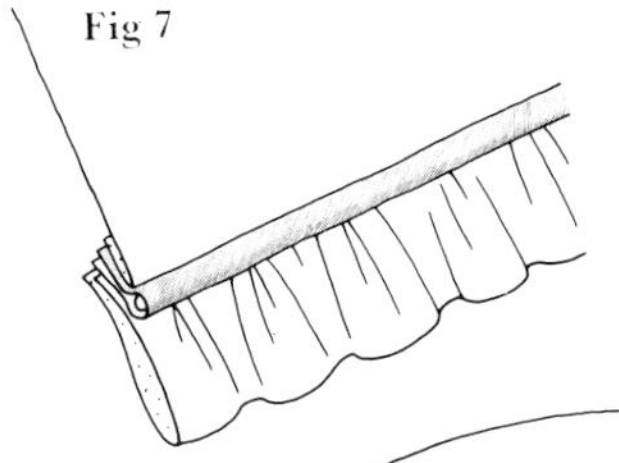

Fig 8

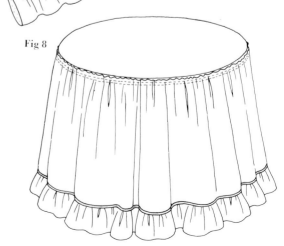

Remove the lower line of gathering stitches. Neaten seam allowances and press upwards (fig 7).

9 Fold over 3.5 cm (1⅜ in) to the wrong side at the top of the skirt and press into position all round. Divide into four sections and run gathering stitches along the skirt top as before, making the lines of stitching 6 mm (¼ in) and 12 mm (½ in) down from the top fold.

10 Divide the circumference of the top piece in four with pins. With right sides uppermost and the fold of the skirt lined up with the top section seam allowance, gather up the skirt to fit the corresponding top sections. Pin and baste in place along the gathering stitches. Then topstitch just above each line of gathering stitches to set the skirt firmly in place. Remove the gathering/basting stitches (fig 8).

11 Turn the tablecloth to the wrong side and neaten the raw edges at the top. Press.

SIMPLE RECTANGULAR TABLECLOTH

Measuring and cutting out

1 Measure across the table top both ways, from A to B and C to D (fig 9). Now measure the drop you require, C to E, and add double this measurement plus 15 cm (6 in) for the hem to both A–B and C–D (fig 10).

Making up

2 If the width of the rectangle amounts to more than the width of your fabric,

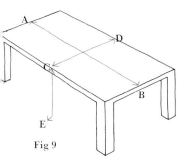

Fig 9

Fig 10

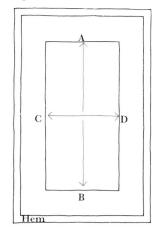

Hem

then widths have to be joined to make up the complete cloth, using flat fell seams (*see page 140*). See steps 2 to 4 of measuring and cutting for round tablecloths at the beginning of the section for details on calculating the amount of fabric you require and making up the basic cloth.

Turning up the hem

3 When you have cut out and/or made up your cloth, press 3 cm ($1\frac{1}{4}$ in) to the wrong side along all edges. Turn in 3 cm ($1\frac{1}{4}$ in) again and press to make a double hem.

4 Mitre the corners (*see page 141*). Baste the hem in place along the inner folded edge. With the right side of the cloth facing upwards, topstitch along the hem just inside the basting stitches. Press, and remove basting.

BEDCOVERINGS

LINED BEDSPREAD

You will need
Fabric
Lining
Tailor's chalk
Dinner plate

Measuring and cutting out

1 Measure the width, A–B, and length, C–D, of the bed with all the usual bedclothes and pillows in place. Allow for any tuck-under at the front and back edges of the pillows and add this allowance on to the length (fig **1a**).

Fig 1a

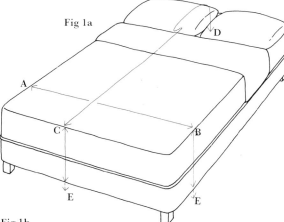

Fig 1b

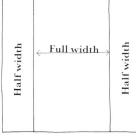

Half width | Full width | Half width

Fig 2

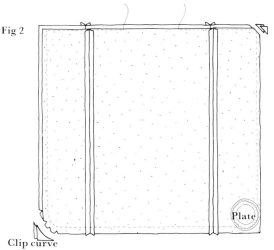

Plate

Clip curve

2 Measure the depth of the overhang at the sides, B–E. A bedspread usually reaches the floor, but if it is to be combined with a valance (dust ruffle), the bedspread should finish just below the valance (dust ruffle) top. Add the E–F measurement to C–D and double this amount to B–E. Then add a seam allowance of 1.5 cm ($\frac{5}{8}$ in) to all edges to obtain the total length and width measurements of the bedspread.

3 To cover anything but a very narrow bed, widths of fabric have to be joined down the long edges to make up the bed width. Joins on the cover should be set to either side of a central strip that runs the length of the bed (fig **1b**). Allow 1.5 cm ($\frac{5}{8}$ in) for seams. If possible, seams should be positioned at

the edges of the bed. Add the depth of one pattern repeat to the total amount required if matching patterns across seams (*see page 95*, step 8).

4 Cut out the required number of fabric and lining pieces to the correct size: one centre panel and two side sections in both fabric and lining if you are joining panels of fabric to make up the total bedspread width.

Making up

5 Make up the fabric and lining pieces if necessary. With right sides together and raw edges even, attach one side section to either side of the central panel. Press the seam allowances open.

6 Set the fabric over the lining with right sides together, matching raw edges and seams. Pin along edges.

7 Next round off the bottom edges of the bedspread if you wish. Position a dinner plate with its edges level with the raw edges of the fabric and lining (fig **2**). Draw round the plate with tailor's chalk and repeat at the other corner. Cut along the curved line.

8 Stitch all round the bedspread, taking a 1.5 cm ($\frac{5}{8}$ in) seam allowance and leaving a central gap of about 60 cm (24 in) at the top edge of the bedspread through which to turn (fig 2). Trim the top corners and clip the curves at 1.5 cm ($\frac{5}{8}$ in) intervals. Turn and press.

9 Turn in opening edges in line with remainder of the seam and slipstitch (*see page 140*) to close.

FITTED AND PIPED BEDSPREAD WITH PILLOW GUSSETS AND KICK PLEATS

You will need
Fabric
Contrast fabric for the piping bias strips (*see page 140*)
Pre-shrunk piping cord
Pattern paper

Measuring and cutting out

1 Measure for this bedspread with the normal bedclothes and pillows in place. First measure the

width, A–B, and the length C–D. Measure the overhang C–E, and the length of the sides, F–G. Measure from H to I, beginning at the back edge of the bed and finishing 10 cm (4 in) beyond the front edge of the pillow (fig 3). Finally measure the depth of the pillows, H–J.

2 Cut one piece of fabric for the bed top to the correct width and length, adding a 5 cm (2 in) hem allowance at the top end and 1.5 cm ($\frac{5}{8}$ in) to the three remaining edges for seams. You will not be able to cover the top of a made-up standard double bed with one width of 137 cm (54 in) wide fabric. In this case, position a panel of fabric down the centre of the cover with narrower panels set to either side (fig 3). Extra fabric should be allowed for matching patterns across seams (*see page 95, step 8*).

3 Add twice the side measurement F–G to the width A–B. Cut enough skirt strips to equal this distance when joined, adding 10 cm (4 in) for side hems, 40.5 cm (16 in) for each pleat, and 1.5 cm ($\frac{5}{8}$ in) seam allowance for each end to be joined. The strip width should equal E–F plus 6.5 cm (2$\frac{5}{8}$ in). Allow extra fabric for pattern matching across seams if necessary.

4 Make a wedge-shaped paper pattern to the pillow gusset measurements, adding a seam allowance of 1.5 cm ($\frac{5}{8}$ in) all round. Cut two gusset pieces.

5 Cut enough contrast bias strips (*see page 140*) to cover the required length of piping cord when joined.

Making up

6 Make up (*see page 141*) enough covered piping to fit around the bed and gusset.

7 Round off the top outer corner of each gusset wedge. The rim of a small glass gives the right amount of curve. With raw edges even, pin the piping to the right side of the fabric along the top of each gusset around the curve and along the inner edge to the inner point. Push back the covering for 1.5 cm ($\frac{5}{8}$ in) at each end and cut away the cord, thus avoiding bulk in the seams. Baste.

8 With right sides together and raw edges even, stitch the pillow gussets to the top section of the bedspread, easing the fabric to fit and leaving 5 cm (2 in) free at the central section top edge for the hem (fig 4).

9 Round off the bottom corners of the top section in the same way as for

the gussets. Pin the piping to the right side of the top section along the edges, starting at the back edge of one pillow gusset and continuing round to the back edge of the other. Trim away the cord for 1.5 cm ($\frac{5}{8}$ in) as in step 7 at each gusset back edge. Baste.

10 Join the skirt strips. Turn 2.5 cm (1 in) to the wrong side twice to make double hems along the side edges and base, folding mitred corners (*see page 141*). Hem by hand or machine in place.

11 With right sides together and raw edges even, lining up the skirt side with the gusset back seam allowance, begin pinning and basting the skirt to the top section over the piping cord. Fold an inverted pleat (fig 5) at each corner at the bed base end. Stitch. Neaten seams (*see page 117*) and clip curves.

12 Turn under 2.5 cm (1 in) twice at the top of the bedspread to make a double hem. Hem by hand or machine in place.

13 Press the pleats and hems to finish.

LINED FITTED BEDSPREAD WITH PILLOW GUSSETS AND SCALLOPED EDGE

This bedspread is used with a valance (dust ruffle), the scalloped edge overlapping the valance (dust ruffle) top. The skirt has corner seams and each side section consists of two widths of fabric that have been joined to make up the length of the bed (about 200 cm/6 feet). Cut one full width and one half width strip for each side from 137 cm (54 in) wide fabric and trim to fit. The join should be positioned nearest the bed foot. Patterns should match across seams and line up around the bed if a fabric with a bold design has been used such as the one on page 55. Add the depth of three vertical pattern repeats to the total fabric amount to allow for this. (*See page 95 step 8.*)

If your fabric is not wide enough for you to cut the bedspread end in one piece, you can wrap the side pieces around the corners. In this

case position the side joins nearest the top of the bed so you can match the pattern across the seams at the end of the bed.

You will need
Fabric
Lining
Length of card from which to cut template

Measuring and cutting out

1 Measure the bed as in step 1 of the previous instructions. Follow steps 2 and 4 to cut out the top section and gusset pieces from both the fabric and lining, but allow 20 cm (8 in) at the top edge of the bed top section instead of 5 cm (2 in).

2 From the fabric cut the widths to make up each side section, following the notes given above. When joined, each side section should measure G–H plus 5 cm (2 in) for the side hem and 1.5 cm ($\frac{5}{8}$ in) for the corner seam. The depth should equal E–F plus 6.5 cm (2$\frac{5}{8}$ in). Cut one end section that measures A–B plus 3 cm (1$\frac{1}{4}$ in) by E–F plus 6.5 cm (2$\frac{5}{8}$ in). Repeat to cut out the lining pieces.

Making up

3 Taking the fabric pieces first, attach the pillow gussets to the top section as in step 8 of the previous instructions. Repeat to make up the lining pieces.

Join the skirt fabric pieces in the right order to make a continuous length, matching patterns across seams and taking a 1.5 cm ($\frac{5}{8}$ in) seam allowance. Repeat to join the skirt lining pieces. Press all seams open.

4 With right sides together lay the skirt fabric length over the lining, matching raw edges and seams. Baste together along the length about 10 cm (4 in) up from the bottom edge, keeping the bottom raw edges even.

5 Make a template for the scallops out of card First divide each side of the bedspread into equal sized scallops. Decide on the approximate width of the scallop and then divide the finished width of the bed-

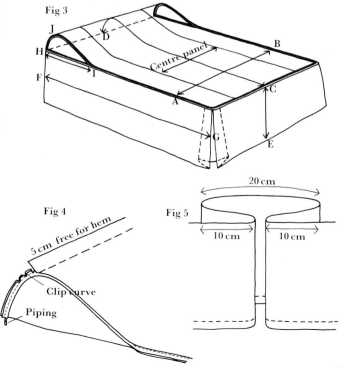

Fig 3

Fig 4

5 cm free for hem

Clip curve

Piping

Fig 5

20 cm

10 cm   10 cm

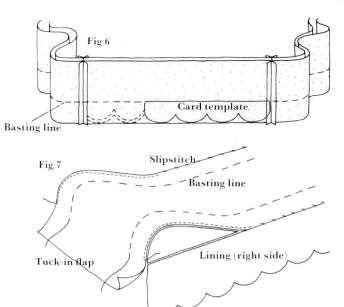

Fig 6

Card template.

Basting line

Fig 7

Slipstitch

Basting line

Tuck-in flap

Lining (right side)

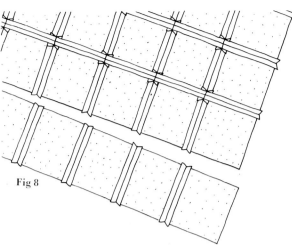

Fig 8

spread by this amount. Juggle with the width measurement until you end up with a round number. (It is more important to fit a round number of scallops into the width than it is the length.)

6 Make a card template for the scallops. Take a convenient length of card (eg four times the scallop length) a little wider than the proposed depth of your scallop and divide it into evenly sized shapes, drawing round a plate as a guide. Cut round the scallops.

7 Lining up the deepest part of the scallop curves with the skirt base edge, draw round template, working out from corner seams to mark scallops along entire base edge. Make sure a round number of scallops fits into bedspread width (fig 6).

8 Baste round the scallops just inside the marked line to hold. Stitch round the scallops, taking a 1.5 cm ($\frac{5}{8}$ in) hem allowance. Trim the seam allowances to 1 cm ($\frac{3}{8}$ in). Clip into the seam allowances at the points of the scallops to ease, and along the curved edges.

9 Join the fabric and lining lengths at both ends, taking a 1.5 cm ($\frac{5}{8}$ in) seam allowance. Turn to the right side and press. With raw edges even, pin the fabric and lining together along the top to hold.

10 With right sides together and raw edges even, baste the lined skirt to the fabric top section, matching side edges and corners to the appropriate seamlines. Stitch. Press the seam allowances upwards.

11 With right sides together and raw edges even, join the lining to the top section along the three edges of the 20 cm (8 in) top flap, taking a 1.5 cm ($\frac{5}{8}$ in) seam allowance.

12 Turn the lining to the wrong side of the bedspread, matching seams. Baste the lining in position along the bedspread top about 5 cm (2 in) in from the sides (fig 7). At each side stitch around the curved edge of the gusset through all thicknesses about 3 mm ($\frac{1}{8}$ in) from the seam. Turn under 1.5 cm ($\frac{5}{8}$ in) along the lining raw edges and slipstitch (see page 140) to the skirt along the seamline, enclosing the raw edges of the top section and skirt.

PATCHWORK BEDSPREAD WITH DIAGONAL QUILTING

This bedspread is much simpler to make than it looks. The most time-consuming element is the quilting. The patchwork is quilted by stitching it to a layer of wadding (batting) backed with muslin; its edges wrap round to the underside of the wadding layer which is lined. Allowance must be made for shrinkage when quilting as the rows of

stitches draw the fabric into the wadding (batting). A rough guide when using 4 oz wadding (medium loft batting) is to allow 2.5 cm (1 in) for shrinkage for every 30 cm (12 in) of fabric/wadding (batting)/lining, and it is better to err on the generous side. The finished patchwork squares in these instructions measure 8 cm by 8 cm ($3\frac{1}{4}$ in by $3\frac{1}{4}$ in).

You will need

Cotton lawn (percale) or equivalent lightweight fabric in five different prints

Lining

4 oz washable synthetic wadding (medium loft batting or polyester fiberfill quilt batt)

Lightweight muslin for backing

Matching or contrast thread for quilting

Metre/yard stick

Tailor's chalk

Measuring and cutting out

1 Measure for the bedspread as explained in lined bedspread steps 1 and 2, omitting the seam allowances.

2 Calculate how many 8 cm by 8 cm ($3\frac{1}{4}$ in by $3\frac{1}{4}$ in) squares will be needed to make up the bedspread. Add on two extra rows (more if you are making a very large bedspread) of patches at each side to allow for turn-under and shrinkage. Divide this amount by five to find out how many squares in each print you need. Next add on a seam allowance of 1 cm ($\frac{3}{8}$ in) all round the square for joins, giving a cutting dimension of 10 cm by 10 cm (4 in by 4 in). You will be able to fit 9 squares across 90 cm (36 in) wide fabric. Calculate how many rows of squares you need in each print

and multiply by 10 cm (4 in) to obtain the length of fabric required. Skip step 3 if using a quilt batt.

3 If necessary, cut enough widths of wadding (batting) to make up the total finished width of the patchwork when joined minus 1 row of squares at each side. (Wadding (batting) is usually 90 cm/36 in wide.) The length of each wadding (batting) width should measure the total finished length of the patchwork minus 1 row of squares at each end. The long edges are butted together and secured with herringbone stitches (see step 6), so there is no need to include a seam allowance for joins.

4 Cut the muslin to the same dimensions as the wadding (batting) lengths. The lining should be cut when you have completed the quilting.

Making up

5 Begin joining the squares into long strips measuring the length of the bedspread. Attach the squares in random order to give the quilt this effect when it is made up. Make up enough strips to obtain the bedspread width when joined together. Press the seams open and attach the strip lengths to each other down the long edges until you have built up the bedspread width. Try not to put two of the same print squares together. Press the seams (fig 8). Skip step 6 if using a quilt batt.

6 Butt the long edges of the wadding (batting) lengths against each other.

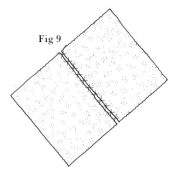

Fig 9

Herringbone stitch (*see page 139*) together across the gap down the back and front of the wadding (batting) to join, taking largish stitches (fig **9**).

7 Lay the patchwork out flat with the right side uppermost. Using the metre/ yard stick and tailor's chalk mark a diagonal line from corner to corner. Working out from the centre, continue marking parallel diagonal lines 2.5 cm (1 in) apart until you have covered the bedspread. Draw a diagonal line to join the remaining corners and mark across the bedspread in the same way to form a diagonal grid.

8 Set the wadding (batting) centrally against the wrong side of the patchwork and lay the muslin over the top. Pin together, starting in the middle and working outwards. Baste across and down the bedspread at 15 cm (6 in) intervals, then baste diagonally across at the same intervals.

9 Make up a small sandwich of fabric, wadding (batting) and muslin backing. Using this as a test piece, stitch a few rows of quilting to check the tension of your machine and ascertain the most suitable stitch length.

10 Machine stitch along the diagonal lines through all layers to quilt the patchwork.

11 Turn the unstitched border of squares to the back of the bedspread, folding mitred corners (*see page 141*). Pin and then herringbone stitch loosely to the wadding (batting) and backing to secure.

12 Next cut out the lining. This should equal the square/rectangle of wadding (batting) and backing showing on the underside of the bed-

spread plus an allowance of 5 cm (2 in) all round. Join lengths of fabric if necessary to make up the overall width (see lined bedspread, step 3), taking a 1.5 cm (⅝ in) seam allowance. Press under the edges of the lining by 2.5 cm (1 in) all round.

13 With the bedspread laid out flat, the back uppermost, mark parallel lines down the unlined wadding (batting) backing section about 30 cm (12 in) apart, beginning at the bedspread centre and working outwards. Place the lining centrally over this unlined area and lockstitch (*see page 140*) it in place down the marked rows (*see page 98, step 7*), working from the centre outwards and beginning and ending the stitching 2.5 cm (1 in) from the patchwork edges.

14 Slipstitch (*see page 140*) the lining to the patchwork all round the edges.

PATCHWORK BEDSPREAD

This patchwork bedspread has a double border and is made up of 25 cm by 5 cm (10 in by 2 in) rectangles (finished dimensions) randomly arranged in sets of five different prints that are stitched together to form a 25 cm by 25 cm (10 in by 10 in) square. The outer border is 15 cm (6 in) wide and the inner 7.5 cm (3 in) wide. The bedspread can be quilted, following the previous instructions (see step 13 below for details). As there are very few lines of quilting no allowance need be made for shrinkage. The bedspread is lined.

You will need
Cotton lawn (percale) in five
   different prints
Lining
For optional quilting: 4 oz
   washable synthetic wadding
   (medium loft batting or
   polyester fiberfill quilt batt)
Lightweight muslin backing,
   matching or contrasting
   thread for quilting

Measuring and cutting out
1 Measure for the bedspread as explained in steps 1 and 2 of the lined bedspread instructions (*see page 125*), omitting to add the seam allowance.

2 Subtract twice the total width of the two borders from the bedspread length and width dimensions to obtain the dimensions of the patchwork section. Calculate how many 25 cm by 25 cm (10 in by 10 in) squares will fit into this section. As you are unlikely to obtain a round number, you can either round up or down to make the bedspread slightly larger or smaller or change the rectangle or border size to fit.

3 Add 1 cm (⅜ in) seam allowance all round the rectangle dimensions to give a cutting dimension of 27 cm by 7 cm (10¾ in by 2¾ in). Calculate how many rectangles will fit lengthways across your chosen fabric width. Divide the total rectangle amount required in one print by this number to find the number of rows of rectangles you need and multiply this by the rectangle width to get the total amount of fabric needed. (For example: 144 squares means you need 144 rectangles in one of the five prints. Three 27 cm by 7 cm (10¾ in by 2¾ in) rectangles fit lengthways into a width of 90 cm (36 in) fabric. 14 divided by 3 equals 48 rows. 48 times 7 cm (2¾ in) equals 336 cm/132 in). Cut the required amount of rectangles to the correct size.

4 For the inner border panel cut two strips of 9.5 cm (3¾ in) wide fabric measuring the length of the inner patchwork section plus 19 cm (7½ in) and mark them A. Cut another two 9.5 cm (3¾ in) wide strips measuring the width of the bedspread plus 19 cm (7½ in) and mark them B. For the outer border panel cut two strips of 17 cm (6¾ in) wide fabric measuring the length of one of an A strip plus 34 cm (13½ in). In the same fabric cut another two 17 cm (6¾ in) wide strips measuring the length of a B strip plus 34 cm (13½ in).

5 Cut the lining to the finished bedspread dimensions plus 1 cm (⅜ in) seam allowance all round.

6 If you are quilting the bedspread cut the wadding (batting) and backing to

the finished dimensions of the bedspread leaving off the seam allowance. (See steps 3 and 6 of the previous instructions if you need to join widths of wadding (batting) to gain the full width of the bedspread.)

Making up
7 With right sides together and raw edges even, randomly attach the fabric rectangles along the long edges to form sets of five, taking a 1 cm (⅜ in) seam allowance.

8 Make up these five-rectangle squares into a strip measuring the desired length of the patchwork section, placing the squares so that the rectangles alternate horizontally and vertically (fig **10**).

9 Continue making strips until you have enough to make up the width of the patchwork section. Be careful to begin each strip with the rectangles placed in the opposite direction to those at the beginning of the previous strip, so that the sets of rectangles will alternate vertically and horizontally across the bedspread as well as down the length. Press the seams open. Join the strips together down the long edges, taking a 1 cm (⅜ in) seam allowance. Press. Set the patchwork section aside.

10 Next join the inner border strips at the corners to make a square/rectangle. At each end of each strip fold up the short raw edge to the opposite long raw edge and press (fig **11**). Unfold and cut along the crease line.

11 Take the strips and place the angled edges together, raw edges even, right sides facing. (Make sure you place them in the appropriate order if you are stitching a rectangle.) Stitch across the ends, leaving 1 cm (⅜ in) unstitched at the inner and outer corner (fig **12**). Repeat this process with the outer border strips, leaving 1 cm (⅜ in) unstitched at the inner corners only.

12 With raw edges even and right sides together join the inner border to the

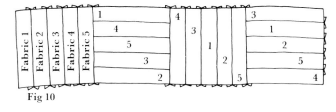

Fig 10

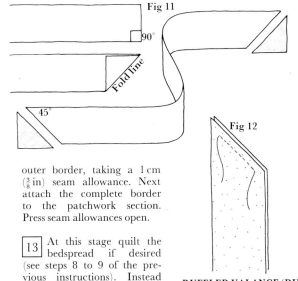

Fig 11

90°

Fold line

45°

Fig 12

outer border, taking a 1 cm ($\frac{3}{8}$ in) seam allowance. Next attach the complete border to the patchwork section. Press seam allowances open.

13 At this stage quilt the bedspread if desired (see steps 8 to 9 of the previous instructions). Instead of sewing diagonal lines of quilting stitches, machine slightly to one side of the main vertical and horizontal seamlines joining the squares to form a 25 cm by 25 cm (10 in by 10 in) grid.

14 Stitch round the outer edge of the patchwork section. Stitch to one side of the inner/outer border seam along all sides. Stitch along all edges of outer border 2 cm ($\frac{3}{4}$ in) from raw edges.

15 With right sides together and raw edges even, attach the lining to the bedspread top following steps 8 and 9 of the lined bedspread instructions. If you have quilted the bedspread make sure there is no wadding (batting) included in the seam.

RUFFLED VALANCE (DUST RUFFLE)

A cheap lining fabric is used for the section concealed under the mattress.

You will need
Fabric for valance (dust ruffle)
Lining fabric for bed top section

Measuring and cutting out
1 Measure the bed without the bedding or mattress in place. For the top section measure the width A–B and the length C–D of the bed top adding 1.5 cm ($\frac{5}{8}$ in) seam allowance to the bottom and sides of the section and 2.5 cm (1 in) for turn-under at the top (fig 13). Cut one piece of lining fabric to these measurements. See lined bedspread instructions, step 3 if your bed top

is wider than the width of your fabric.

2 To calculate the finished length of the valance (dust ruffle) multiply the bed length measurement C–D by four and add twice the width A–B. Cut enough strips of fabric, measuring the depth plus 3.5 cm ($1\frac{3}{8}$ in), to equal the finished width when joined, allowing 1.5 cm ($\frac{5}{8}$ in) for seams. Allow extra fabric to match patterns across seams if necessary (*see page 95, step 8*).

Making up
3 Make up the top section if necessary. Curve the corners using the rim of a small glass as a guide. At the top of the section press 6 mm ($\frac{1}{4}$ in) to the wrong side. Turn under 2 cm ($\frac{3}{4}$ in) again and stitch across close to the inner folded edge of the fabric.

4 Join the valance (dust ruffle) strips and press the seams open. At each end of the valance (dust ruffle) turn under the same hem as at the top of the lining section. At the base edge turn 1 cm ($\frac{3}{8}$ in) to the wrong side twice to make a double hem. Press. Hem by hand or machine in place close to the inner folded edge.

5 Measure twice C–D from each end of the valance (dust ruffle) and mark these distances on the valance (dust ruffle) seam allowance with two pins set close together. Divide each of the resultant three sections in half and mark on the seam allowance with two pins.

6 Next mark the sides and bottom of the top lining section halfway along the edges.

7 Gather the valance (dust ruffle) between each set

of pin markers, sewing two lines of gathering stitches 6 mm ($\frac{1}{4}$ in) apart either side of the seamline (*see page 140*).

8 With right sides together, raw ends even, and matching corresponding pins, pin the valance (dust ruffle) to the top section at the pin dividers and gather up the fabric evenly in between. Baste to hold. Stitch all round the valance (dust ruffle), taking a 1.5 cm ($\frac{5}{8}$ in) seam allowance.

9 Neaten the seam allowances (*see page 117*) and press away from top section.

SPLIT VALANCE (DUST RUFFLE) WITH CONTRAST-BORDERED TOP

This valance (dust ruffle) is a suitable compromise when the outer edges of the section that goes under the mattress would be on view but you don't want to waste expensive fabric covering the whole bed top. The border is 15 cm (6 in) wide.

You will need
Fabric for valance (dust ruffle)
Contrast fabric (optional) for top section border
Lining fabric for top section

Measuring and cutting out
1 Measure for the top section as in step 1 of the previous instructions. Deduct 15 cm (6 in) from the length measurement and 30 cm (12 in) from the width. Add 1.5 cm seam allowance to the side and bottom edges and 2 cm ($\frac{3}{4}$ in) to the top (fig **14a**).

2 Cut two 18 cm ($7\frac{1}{4}$ in) wide border strips that measure C–D plus 5 cm (2 in) and 1.5 cm ($\frac{5}{8}$ in) seam allowance. Cut one 18 cm ($7\frac{1}{4}$ in) wide border strip that measures the width A–B plus 3 cm ($1\frac{1}{4}$ in).

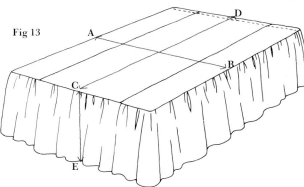

Fig 13

A

D

B

C

E

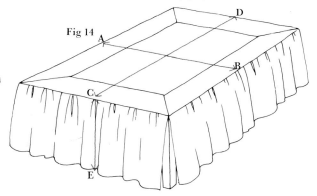

Fig 14

A

D

B

C

E

3 For each valance (dust ruffle) side width cut enough fabric strips, measuring a width of C–E plus 3.5 cm ($1\frac{3}{8}$ in), to equal twice C–D when joined. Allow 1.5 cm ($\frac{5}{8}$ in) at each strip end for joins. Cut enough same width strips to equal A–B when joined.

Making up

4 Join the three border strips as in steps 9 and 10 of patchwork bedspread instructions, taking 1.5 cm ($\frac{5}{8}$ in) seam allowance, leaving 1.5 cm ($\frac{5}{8}$ in) unstitched at bottom inner corners.

5 Right sides together, raw edges even, join border to centre section. Turn 1 cm ($\frac{3}{8}$ in) to the wrong side twice at top of the centre section to make a double hem. Stitch across the top close to inner folded edge.

6 Join strips to make up side and bed end sections of the valance (dust ruffle). Turn under 1 cm ($\frac{3}{8}$ in) twice to make double hems at the ends of each valance (dust ruffle) section. Press. Hem by hand or machine stitch. Turn under 1 cm ($\frac{3}{8}$ in) twice along base of each section. Press and stitch.

7 Divide each valance (dust ruffle) section in half and mark on the seam allowance with two pins set close together. Gather and attach the valance as in steps 6 to 9 of the previous instructions, matching the splits in the valance (dust ruffle) with the top section corners.

8 At the corner splits slip-stitch (*see page 140*) the edges together for 1.5 cm ($\frac{5}{8}$ in) down from the valance (dust ruffle) top to neaten.

FITTED QUILTED BEDSPREAD WITH CONTRAST PIPING
(single bed size)

This bedspread overlaps the top of the valance (dust ruffle). The pattern has been picked out with quilting stitches.

You will need
Fabric
Lining for top section
Contrast fabric for piping bias strips (*see page 140*)
Pre-shrunk piping cord
4 oz washable synthetic wadding (medium loft batting or polyester fiberfill quilt batt)
Lightweight muslin backing for wadding (batting)
Matching or contrasting thread for quilting

Measuring and cutting out

1 Measure the length and width of the bed with its normal bedding in place (fig **15**). To the length measurement C–D add 20 cm (8 in) for tuck-in at the top of the bed plus 1.5 cm ($\frac{5}{8}$ in) seam allowance and 20 cm (8 in) to allow for shrinkage while quilting (see the introduction of patchwork bedspread with diagonal quilting). To width add 3 cm ($1\frac{1}{4}$ in) for seams plus 15 cm (6 in) shrinkage allowance.

2 Read through paragraph one of the introduction to the lined fitted bedspread with scalloped edge instructions. You may wish to cut the side sections on the length of the fabric. Whichever way you choose to cut the fabric, the side sections should measure the depth C–E plus 12 cm (5 in) hem, seam and quilting shrinkage allowance by the length C–D plus 25 cm (10 in) side hem, seam and shrinkage allowance. Cut one end piece to measure the depth C–E plus 15 cm (6 in) by the width A–B plus 23 cm (9 in) seam and shrinkage allowance.

3 Cut the one piece of wadding (batting) and one piece of backing to the dimensions of the bed top piece. You may have to join lengths of wadding (batting) to gain the width of the bedspread top. See page 127 step 3 for details. Cut the wadding (batting) and backing side and end sections to the same dimensions as the fabric sections.

4 Cut the lining to the dimensions of the bed top section minus 15 cm (6 in) on the width and 20 cm (8 in) on the length.

5 For each pleat cut a rectangle of fabric measuring 44 cm ($17\frac{1}{4}$ in) wide by C–E plus 6.5 cm ($2\frac{5}{8}$ in) long.

6 Cut enough contrast bias strips to cover the piping cord when joined.

Making up

7 To attach the backing and wadding (batting) to each fabric piece follow steps 8 and 9 of the patchwork quilt with diagonal quilting.

8 Decide on the areas of the print you wish to feature, then beginning with a side skirt section stitch around the flowers, leaves and stalks, starting at the centre of the piece of fabric and working outwards. At the end of a section of pattern leave enough thread to be pulled through to the inside and tied off invisibly. Repeat to quilt each section.

9 When the quilting has been completed remove the basting and cut each piece to the correct size, following the measurements given above MINUS the shrinkage allowances. Curve

Fig 16

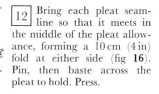
Unquilted pleat section

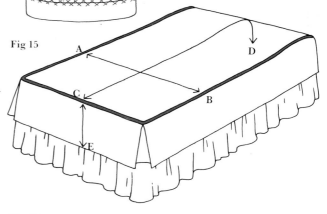
Fig 15

the bottom corners of the top section using the rim of a small glass to give a neat outline. Next trim the wadding (batting) from the hem and seam allowances.

10 With right sides together and raw edges even, join one kick pleat section to a side section at the bottom end, and to the end piece at the other side, taking a 1.5 cm ($\frac{5}{8}$ in) seam allowance. Repeat, to join the other pleat section. Press the seam allowances flat on to each main section.

11 Neaten (*see page 117*) the side and base edges of the skirt/pleat strip and then turn under a 5 cm (2 in) hem, mitring the outer corners (*see page 141*). Herringbone stitch (*see page 139*) the side and base hem to the wadding (batting) all round the bedspread to secure.

12 Bring each pleat seamline so that it meets in the middle of the pleat allowance, forming a 10 cm (4 in) fold at either side (fig **16**). Pin, then baste across the pleat to hold. Press.

Fig 17

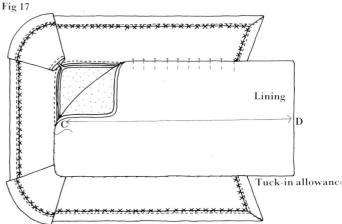
Lining
Tuck-in allowance

13 Make up enough covered piping (*see page 141*) to go round the bed as indicated in fig **15**. With raw edges even baste it to the right side of the top section around three edges.

14 With raw edges even and right sides together attach the lining to the edges of the tuck-in allowance. Clip across the corners and turn the lining to the inside. Press.

15 With raw edges even and right sides together pin and baste the skirt to the top section, positioning a pleat at each bottom corner. Stitch, using the zipper foot on the machine. Press the seam allowances upwards and clip the corner curves.

16 Turn under 1.5 cm ($\frac{5}{8}$ in) along the edges of the lining and slipstitch (*see page 140*) it to the skirt/top section seamline to secure (fig **17**). Press.

LINED BEDSPREAD WITH QUILTED DRAGON PANELS

This bedspread makes very creative use of Opium from the East India collection, available in 137 cm (54 in) width. The finished length of the bedspread is 265 cm (104 in) and the width 233 cm (91$\frac{1}{2}$ in). It is made of two separate halves joined together down the centre of the bedspread and bound at top and bottom to finish (fig **18**).

You will need
Fabric equal to twice the quilt length plus 53 cm (21 in) for quilting shrinkage (see introduction to patchwork bedspread with diagonal quilting), 6 cm (2$\frac{1}{2}$ in) for seams, and a pattern repeat allowance (*see page 95*, step 8) plus 80 cm (31$\frac{1}{2}$ in) for top and bottom binding. The stripes and border from this section are pieced together for the correct binding length, and main panels used for matching cushions.
Lining fabric to the same length as the fabric minus the pattern repeat allowance and binding allowance. (Here Suki from the East India Collection has been used.)
4 oz washable synthetic wadding (medium loft batting or polyester fiberfill quilt batt)

Measuring and cutting out
1 Cut out the top fabric, firstly dividing it into two equal lengths, then closely following figs **18** and **19**, showing the cutting lines along the stripes. Set aside the central border strip not needed now, since this will form the backing strip for the top and bottom binding.

Making up
2 Taking one cut length, set each cut stripe section, all right sides uppermost, against its neighbour as shown in figs **18** and **19**, folding seam allowances of between 0.5 cm ($\frac{1}{4}$ in) and 1 cm ($\frac{3}{8}$ in) to the inside, and pin and baste into position. Edgestitch from top to bottom (fig **20**,) down each join.

3 Repeat step 2 for the other cut length of top fabric, then matching up the print repeat of each dragon with the stitched half-cover, trim away superfluous fabric to create two equal halves of the cover. Do not trim away selvedges, since these will form valuable seam allowances at a later stage.

4 Cut the wadding (batting) into two equal lengths and set behind each top half of the bedspread, which should now measure a width of 119 cm (46$\frac{3}{4}$ in) inclusive of seam allowances at centre and selvedge. Match up the outside edges of both wadding (batting) and top fabric, allowing it to extend beyond the fabric at the centre of each half cover. This extension will be lapped and joined later on. Pin temporarily into position, working from the centre outwards, then set one lining length behind the wadding (batting), wrong side to wadding (batting), so that the wadding (batting) forms a sandwich centre between the two layers of fabric. Match outside edges of wadding (batting) and lining fabric, and leave inner, central side untrimmed.

5 Now pin, then baste into position at 10 cm (4 in) intervals, across and down each half cover, starting in the centre and working outwards until the whole length of each piece is set lightly into position. Then baste each half cover dia-

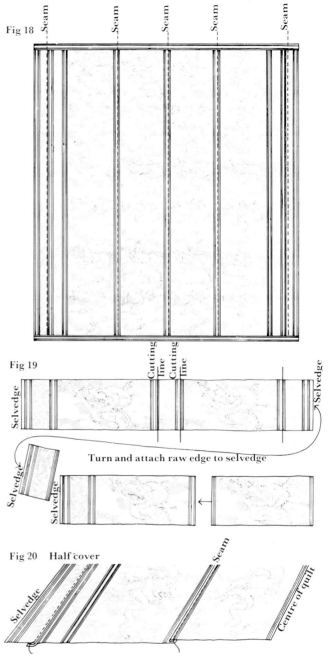

Fig 18   Seam   Seam   Seam   Seam   Seam

Fig 19   Cutting line   Cutting line   Selvedge   Selvedge

Selvedge   Selvedge

Turn and attach raw edge to selvedge

Fig 20   Half cover   Seam   Centre of quilt   Selvedge

gonally at the same intervals. (This is time-consuming, but if it is not done as described, the danger of fabric moving during stitching process increases; the cover will be lumpy and uneven, and the pattern will not match.)

6 To quilt, firstly stitch a small leftover sample of the thicknesses together to check tension and a medium stitch length. Now begin with one half cover by firstly stitching down each side of the 6-stripe panels, along the edge of each outer stripe, working from the centre, first down and then up, to each raw edge, and through all thicknesses. Do not stitch the outer stripe on each side of the half cover. Repeat for the other half cover.

7 For the dragon panels, follow the print lines of each dragon, beginning with the central one, and starting at his head, stitch around his flames, teeth, front foot and claws and continue down the body, stitching around each important part of the print. Complete the stitching up his back and around the feet and claws, to finish where you began. Pull threads to the lining side and neaten. Repeat

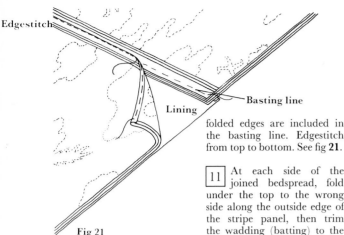

Edgestitch

Lining

Basting line

Fig 21

for each dragon, then stitch around outside of each cloud, neatening ends.

8 Repeat for the other half cover, then remove all basting stitches.

9 To join the two halves of the quilt, lay them right sides uppermost, flat in front of you, then fold under a seam allowance at the centre of the left half cover of both top and lining fabric edges to the wrong side. Trim the wadding (batting) in the middle of the left half cover to come even with the folded edges, then wrapping the top fabric over the wadding's (batting's) raw edge, baste each fold into position from top to bottom. Make sure the fold line of the top fabric is basted so that it will exactly follow the stripe pattern of two sets of three stripes each, with a small gap in the middle, when joined to the other side. Leave right half cover unfolded.

10 On the right half cover, trim the wadding (batting) to the same width as the unfolded edges, then baste top and lining fabric and wadding (batting), together. Turning back the basted edges of the left half cover out of the way, insert the right half cover's basted edge into the left half cover's centre, setting the folded edges of the left half cover over and under the right half cover, to enclose it. Now with stripe pattern in place on top of the cover, pin, then baste the two halves together, enclosing raw edges and basting into position close to the folded edges and through all thicknesses, making sure both

folded edges are included in the basting line. Edgestitch from top to bottom. See fig **21**.

11 At each side of the joined bedspread, fold under the top to the wrong side along the outside edge of the stripe panel, then trim the wadding (batting) to the same width as the folded line. Unfold the top fabric and refold, wrapping over the wadding's (batting's) raw edge and baste into position. Fold under lining fabric equal to the fold of the top fabric, then baste both fabrics together. Edgestitch from top to bottom, and repeat for the other side.

12 To 'top and tail' the bedspread with the striped binding, cut widths of stripe from the 80 cm ($31\frac{3}{8}$ in) length of fabric set aside, allowing 1 cm ($\frac{3}{8}$ in) seam allowances on each side. Join these strips, matching stripes, right sides together, to equal two lengths of the width of the bedspread, plus seam allowances of 3 cm ($1\frac{1}{4}$ in). Cut similar strips from the left-over central border of top fabric. Press seam allowances open.

13 Join one stripe to one border strip, right sides together along one long edge, and stitch from end to end, taking a 1 cm ($\frac{3}{8}$ in) seam allowance. Press seam allowances open, then fold under 1 cm ($\frac{3}{8}$ in) at remaining raw edges of the binding strip thus formed, to the wrong side, and wrap over the raw edge of the top of the cover, stripe to topside, border print to lining underside, so that raw edges are enclosed and butt up to the seamline joining the two sections of binding together. Baste into position along the edges of the folds, including underneath folded edge in the basting line, and tucking under seam allowances at each end, to the inside. Edgestitch all the way along, through all thicknesses and round short ends to close. Repeat for bottom of quilt to finish.

MISCELLANEOUS

GATHERED TENTED CEILING

This tented ceiling is not what it seems. It has been gathered to the centre top of a mirrored wall, rather than to the middle of a room, but the reflection of the half ceiling in the mirror gives the illusion of a complete ceiling and a room that is twice the size. The following instructions are for a complete tented ceiling as it is unlikely that most people will have the requisite mirrored wall to make the half version effective. A fabric fullness of two and a half times the total length of the walls was allowed to tent the ceiling on page 70, but one and a half times the wall length will still produce a very attractive result. A vast amount of fabric is required—in the example photographed the room, which is about $3\frac{1}{2}$ metres (12 ft) square, took over 33 metres (36 yards) of fabric.

You will need
Fabric
Four 2 cm by 4 cm ($\frac{3}{4}$ in by $1\frac{1}{2}$ in) wooden battens the length of each wall
Four 12 mm by 3 cm ($\frac{1}{2}$ in by $1\frac{1}{4}$ in) wooden battens the same length as above
Three 3 cm by 6 mm ($1\frac{1}{4}$ in by $\frac{1}{4}$ in) wooden fillets the same length as above
20 cm (8 in) square wooden ceiling block 2.5 cm (1 in) deep
Screws (including fine screws and ceiling screws), plastic wall plugs, and panel pins
Staple gun
Fabric glue
15.5 cm ($6\frac{1}{4}$ in) diameter heavy cardboard circle
Someone to help you attach the tent

Measuring, cutting out and fixing the wall battens
1 Locate the centre of the ceiling, making sure there is a joist there and checking the position of the wiring. Attach the wooden block centrally to the ceiling at this point. Drill holes across the centre of the block about 5 cm (2 in) apart, then mark and drill corresponding holes in the joist. Insert wall plugs and screw the batten into place.

2 If your room is square measure the length of one of the walls from corner to corner, and the distance from the corner to centre of the wooden block (fig **1**). If your room is rectangular, measure the length of one long and one short wall as well as the distance from the corner to the centre of the wooden block.

3 *For a square room* multiply the wall length by the fabric fullness you require; here $2\frac{1}{2}$ times the length. Divide by the width of your chosen fabric and round up to the nearest width. Multiply this number by the length of the DIAGONAL to find the total amount of fabric you need to cover one wall section of the ceiling and by four to obtain the grand total. *For a rectangular room* repeat these calculations for one short and one long wall, add the two together and multiply by two to obtain the grand total. For each width of fabric required add 15 cm (6 in) to the total length for batten turn-under allowances. If matching patterns, allow 1 pattern repeat measurement per width, minus the first width, adding this calculation to the total.

4 Cut the number of fabric lengths required. Each length should measure the length of the diagonal plus 15 cm (6 in), and separate the number needed for each wall section into four piles.

5 Attach the four thicker battens to the walls with their top edges about 1.5 cm ($\frac{5}{8}$ in) from the ceiling, mitring their corners to fit. Drill holes at equal, 30 cm (12 in) intervals along the wall, insert wall plugs, mark off and drill corresponding holes along the centre of the battens, then screw them into place.

Making up
6 Beginning with one pile of fabric widths, join them together down the long edges to make one giant width, taking 1.5 cm ($\frac{5}{8}$ in) seam allowances. Repeat for

each pile of fabric widths until you have four giant widths of fabric. Leaving the selvedge free for overlap at either side, run two rows of largish gathering stitches along the wall top edge of each fabric section, about 2 cm ($\frac{3}{4}$in) and 3 cm ($1\frac{1}{4}$in) from the edge, breaking the gathering at convenient intervals, with one of the breaks positioned at the centre of the section.

7 | Take one fabric section and gather it up to fit the wall roughly. Next set the fabric against the batten, matching the marked centre point to the centre of the batten length. The right side of the fabric should be set against the batten and the raw edges lined up with the batten top. Set each outer edge of the section tight into the corner and staple, first folding the selvedge to the wrong side. Be careful not to staple too close to the lower edge of the batten or the wood will split. Working from the wall centre outwards continue stapling the

Fig 1

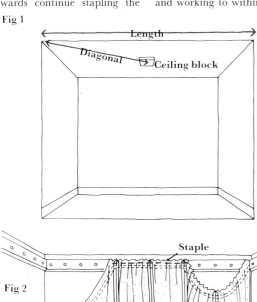

Fig 2

fabric to the batten, adjusting the gathers evenly (fig **2**).

8 | Repeat on the other walls. All four walls should now have a section of gathered fabric dangling down from the batten, wrong sides facing, ready to be attached to the wooden block at the centre of the ceiling.

9 | To secure each fabric section firmly, attach the thinner battens to the first battens over the fabric, lining up base edges and mitring corners (fig **3**). Use finer screws to secure these battens, positioning them at 15 cm (6 in) intervals.

10 | With your helper standing by to hold the fabric, begin attaching one fabric section to the centre block, folding even pleats and pulling the fabric so that it is taut but not too tightly stretched as shown in the photograph on page 70. Staple the pleats into position as you work, flat against the wooden block, trimming the excess fabric and working to within 2.5 cm

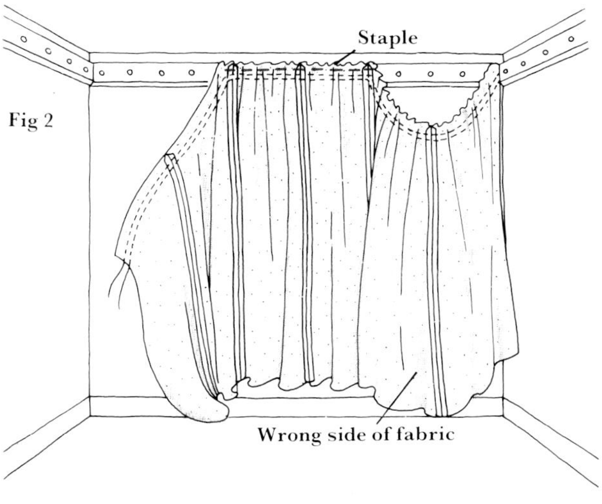

(1 in) of the centre of the block and not further outwards from this point than 6 cm/$2\frac{1}{2}$in (fig **4**). Repeat, to attach the other fabric sections to the wooden block. Make sure there is no gap visible along the diagonal edges where the fabric sections meet.

11 | From the trimmed fabric cut a circle 20 cm (8 in) in diameter. Cover the circular piece of card, overlapping the edges evenly and clipping the seam allowances. Stick it to the underside of the cardboard with glue (fig **5**). Baste round the edges if possible.

12 | While this is drying, make up the choux (the ruffled rose-shaped object set in the middle of the tented ceiling). From the trimmed fabric cut a circle four times the diameter of the glued smaller fabric circle. Run two lines of gathering stitches around the outside of the circle and draw up the gathers tightly, stitching them flat by hand to secure. The circle of fabric formed will now be twice the diameter you require.

13 | Gather and tuck the fabric into ruffled ridges by stabbing the needle and thread through the fabric both vertically and sideways at intervals. The choux should look artfully ruffled rather than mangled when finished, so don't overdo the stabbing.

14 | Position the covered cardboard piece against the ceiling block, centrally over the stapled edges of the fabric. Attach with panel pins. Stitch the finished choux to the fabric circle or staple unobtrusively in place.

15 | Check the length of the fillets along the underside of the battens, mitring the corners to fit. Cover each fillet with a strip of fabric, wrapping it round the fillet to the back, and overlapping edges (fig **6**). Glue or staple to secure the fabric.

16 | Secure each covered fillet in position, flat against the underneath of the battening, butting it up

Fig 3
Cut-away diagram to show layers

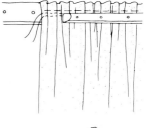

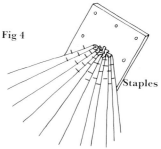

Fig 4

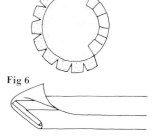

Fig 5

Fig 6

against the wall, so that no wood can be seen. Secure with panel pins evenly spaced along the underside of each fillet.

GATHERED FABRIC WALLS

The fabric covering the angled wall on page 72 has a casing at the top and bottom through which wooden poles are slotted. The third pole, which holds the fabric against the wall angle, has been slotted through a channel stitched halfway down to the back of the fabric. Since the fabric is unlined, two and a half times the width of the wall has been allowed for fullness (see Headings, page 94). If you are using a boldly patterned fabric you may wish to match patterns across seams, even though the covering is very gathered. Extra fabric should therefore be allowed for this. *See page 95, step 8 for details.*

You will need
Fabric
Three (two if you are covering
an ordinary wall) wooden
poles the length of the wall
Brackets to hold the poles
Heavy cord

Measuring and cutting out

1 Fix the poles in position, making sure they can be removed again when attaching the wall covering.

2 Using the cord, measure from just underneath the top pole to the top of the centre pole. Depending on the slant of the wall add a small amount of drape. Note this measurement. Now measure from just beneath the centre pole to just above the bottom one and add this distance to the previous measurement.

3 To the overall length add the pole circumference measurement plus 9 cm ($3\frac{1}{2}$ in) for each casing (at the top and bottom). If you are making a covering for an angled wall add half the pole circumference plus 12 mm ($\frac{1}{2}$ in) to the length. Multiply the number of fabric widths required to cover the wall to find the amount of fabric you need.

4 Cut the required number of widths to the required length.

5 Cut strips of fabric for the centre pole channel that will measure the finished width of the wall covering when joined plus 3 cm ($1\frac{1}{4}$ in). Each strip should measure a width of half the pole circumference plus 4.5 cm ($1\frac{3}{4}$ in).

Making up

6 With right sides together and edges even, join the wall-covering widths, taking a 1.5 cm ($\frac{5}{8}$ in) seam allowance. Press seams open.

7 At each outer edge of the covering turn under 6 mm ($\frac{1}{4}$ in) to the wrong side and press. Turn under a further 1.5 cm ($\frac{5}{8}$ in). Press. Stitch from top to bottom, close to the inner folded edge.

8 At the top of the covering fold over half the pole circumference plus 4.5 cm ($1\frac{3}{4}$ in) to the wrong side.

Press. Turn under 1.5 cm ($\frac{5}{8}$ in) along the long raw edge of the fabric. Press. Stitch across the covering close to the inner folded edge.

9 Measure half the pole circumference plus 12 mm ($\frac{1}{2}$ in) up from this stitching line and stitch across the covering again at this level to form a casing for the pole. Repeat to make a casing for the bottom pole.

10 Make up the channel strip and press open seams. Fold under 1.5 cm ($\frac{5}{8}$ in) along all the edges of the channel strip and press. Stitch across the end to hold.

11 Next lay the covering flat, wrong side uppermost, and measuring from just beneath the lower stitching line of the top casing, mark the top of the centre pole, as previously noted at the side of the covering. Chalk a straight line across the covering at this level to mark the position for the channel top.

12 Lining up the top edge of the channel strip with the chalk line, pin the strip flat to the covering back along both long edges. Stitch in place close to folded edges.

13 Thread each of the poles, adjusting the gathering, and hang the covering in place.

QUILTED MOSES BASKET (BASSINET) WITH MATCHING COVERLET

This pretty covered basket has quilted sides, an unpadded base over which the mattress is set, a deep ruffle at the sides with openings for the handles, and an elasticized rim strip to hold the cover in place.

You will need
Cotton lawn (percale) (Tana
lawn can be bought ready
quilted to save time)
2 oz washable synthetic wadding
(low loft batting)
Lightweight muslin backing
5 cm (2 in) wide broderie
anglaise (eyelet edging)
2.5 cm (1 in) wide ribbon
6 mm ($\frac{1}{4}$ in) wide elastic, the
length of the rim circum-
ference minus 20 cm (8 in)
Pattern paper

Measuring and cutting out

1 Note the measurements of the following (fig **7**): the circumference of the rim, A–C–A; the circumference of the base, B–D–B; the depth of the basket, H–I; the depth of the ruffle plus broderie anglaise (eyelet edging), A–E; the distance between each outer handle edge, F–G.

2 Set a large sheet of paper against the base of the basket. Mark carefully around the edges, then remove the paper and add 1.5 cm ($\frac{5}{8}$ in) seam allowance all round. Cut out the pattern and mark it 'base'.

3 To make a pattern for the quilted sides of the basket on a large sheet of paper, draw a straight line equalling the distance A–C (half the rim circumference). Draw a second line equalling the measurement B–D at the distance A–B below the first. A–C should overshoot B–D equally on each side. Join these lines at the side. Add seam and quilting shrinkage allowance of 3 cm ($1\frac{1}{4}$ in) at the top and bottom and 5 cm (2 in) at each slanted end. Cut out this pattern and mark it 'sides, cut two'.

4 For the ruffle length double A–C and allow a width of A–E plus 2.5 cm (1 in) for seams minus the depth of the broderie anglaise (eyelet edging). Cut a pattern to these measurements and mark it 'half ruffle, cut 2'.

5 For the rim strip cut a pattern that measures A–C plus 3 cm ($1\frac{1}{4}$ in) for seams plus a width of 10 cm (4 in) and mark it 'rim strip, cut 2'.

6 Lastly cut a rectangle of paper 10 cm (4 in) wide by the distance F–G plus 3 cm ($1\frac{1}{4}$ in). Mark it 'handle strip, cut 2'.

7 Cut out all the basket sections from the top fabric (fig **8**). Cut two side sections to the same dimensions as the fabric pieces from the wadding (batting) and backing.

Making up

8 Lay the wadding (batting) over the wrong side of each fabric side section, and

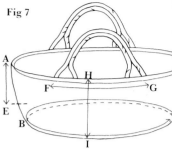

Fig 7

then lay the muslin on top. Beginning at the centre baste the layers together horizontally and vertically at 7.5 cm (3 in) intervals. Next mark the side sections with diagonal quilting lines spaced 2.5 cm (1 in) apart and quilt. (See patchwork bedspread with diagonal quilting, steps 8 and 9.)

9 Trim the quilted side sections to the measurements taken in step 1, allowing 1.5 cm ($\frac{5}{8}$ in) all round for seams. With right sides together and raw edges even, join the side sections together down the short edges. Press the seam allowances open. On the right side of the quilting stitch parallel to the seamline 6 mm ($\frac{1}{4}$ in) to either side to flatten the wadding (batting).

10 With right sides together and raw edges even, join the basket base to the completed side sections, taking a 1.5 cm ($\frac{5}{8}$ in) seam allowance. Clip curves. Oversew (*see page 140*) the seam allowances to neaten (fig **9**).

11 Join the two ruffle strips with French seams (*see page 140*). With right sides together and raw edges even, attach broderie anglaise (eyelet edging) to the lower edge of the ruffle, taking a 6 mm ($\frac{1}{4}$ in) seam allowance. Press the seam allowances upwards and then topstitch along the edge of the fabric, catching in the seam allowances, to set the broderie anglaise (eyelet edging) flat.

12 On the top edge of the ruffle run two rows of gathering stitches either side of the seamline, 6 mm ($\frac{1}{4}$ in) apart.

13 Mark the outside position of the basket handles on the quilted sides with pins, allowing an extra 1.5 cm ($\frac{5}{8}$ in) for ease at each side.

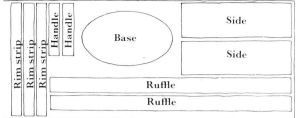

Fig 8

Suggested layout for 90 cm (35 in) wide fabric

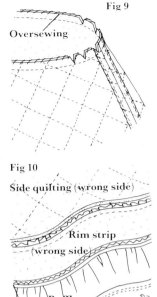

Fig 9

Oversewing

Fig 10

Side quilting (wrong side)

Rim strip (wrong side)

Ruffle

Elastic

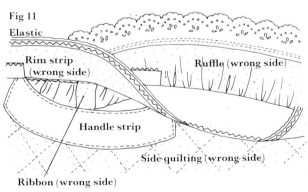

Fig 11

Elastic

Rim strip (wrong side)

Ruffle (wrong side)

Handle strip

Side quilting (wrong side)

Ribbon (wrong side)

Fig 12

Handle opening

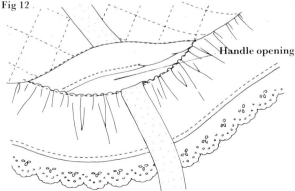

14 With right sides together and raw edges even, position the ruffle against the quilted section of the basket and gather up to fit. Stitch between the pin markers, but do not attach the ruffle to the handle gap section, F–G.

15 Fold under 6 mm (¼ in) along two short sides and one long side of the handle strips. Stitch all round. With right sides together, set the remaining raw edge of each strip against the raw edge of the quilting at the handle position, making sure all the pin markers overlap evenly at each side. Insert a ribbon length in the seam at the centre of the handle section, short raw edge against the quilting edge. Stitch along the length of each handle position through the strip and quilting, taking a 1.5 cm (⅝ in) seam allowance.

16 Turn the strip to the wrong side of the quilting, and then stitch close to the seam on the right side to flatten. Carefully neaten the unstitched side edges. Stitch firmly across each lower corner to secure.

17 With raw edges even and right sides together join the ends of the two rim strips to make a circle. Turn under 6 mm (¼ in) to the wrong side along one long edge and press. Set a piece of elastic twice the length of A–C minus 20 cm (8 in), against this turning and zigzag in position evenly (fig 10), working on half a rim at a time and pulling the elastic gently to ease along the folded edge. Butt the two ends of the elastic neatly together and zigzag firmly across to join (fig 11).

18 With the right side of the rim strip to the wrong side of the ruffle, stitch the rim strip to the ruffle only, just below the first line of stitching. Stitch from outer handle to outer handle, stopping the stitching at the handle opening, F–G.

19 To neaten the handle opening raw edges clip the seam allowance of the rim strip and gathering to just within the stitching line *at the edges of the opening*, then turn the gap *to the right side of the rim strip and wrong side of gathering*. Stitch along the seamline, inserting the other length of ribbon in the middle. Neaten the seam allowances together. On the right side of the ruffle stitch close to the edge from side to side of the handle opening, and across ribbon, to finish. See fig 12.

QUILTED COVERLET

You will need
Fabric
2 oz washable synthetic wadding (low loft batting or polyester fiberfill quilt batt)
Lightweight muslin backing for wadding (batting)
Lining
5 cm (2 in) wide broderie anglaise (eyelet edging)

Making up

1 Take the pattern of the base of the Moses basket (bassinet) left (see step 2) and fold down 10 cm (4 in) evenly at the top of the pattern, pinning down the flap. This gives you the shape of the coverlet. Using this pattern, cut one piece of top fabric, wadding (batting) and backing, adding 2.5 cm (1 in) all round for quilting shrinkage. Cut one piece of lining to the pattern dimensions only.

2 Lay the wadding (batting) over the wrong side of the fabric and place the backing on top of it. Baste the layers together vertically and horizontally at 7.5 cm (3 in) intervals. Mark up with diagonal quilting lines set 2.5 cm (1 in) apart and quilt (see patchwork bedspread with diagonal quilting, steps 8 and 9). Trim cover to pattern dimensions if necessary.

3 Mark a line across the quilt 8 cm (3¼ in) down from the top edge of the quilt. Cut a piece of broderie anglaise (eyelet edging) to fit across the width and neaten (*see page 140*) the raw edge.

4 With right sides together, place the neatened edge against the line marked on the quilt (the scalloped edge will face upwards). Stitch close to the neatened edge. Stitch again 6 mm (¼ in) from the first stitching line. Press the broderie anglaise (eyelet edging) downwards. Stitch across the ends of the broderie anglaise (eyelet edging) 6 mm (¼ in) from the coverlet edges.

5 With right sides together and raw edges matching, pin the lining to the quilt. Stitch all round, leaving a 15 cm (6 in) opening at the bottom of the quilt through which to turn. Trim

the corners, clip curves and turn the coverlet to the right side. Turn in the opening edges in line with the remainder of the seam and slipstitch (*see page 140*) to close (fig **13**).

BASKET WITH QUILTED LINING

This basket is approximately 46 cm (18 in) in diameter at the rim and tapers towards the base. Shrinkage allowance for 2 oz wadding (batting) is about 12 mm ($\frac{1}{2}$ in) for every 30 cm (12 in) of fabric quilted. If your basket is much smaller or larger you can adjust the shrinkage allowance accordingly.

You will need
Fabric
2 oz washable synthetic wadding
   (low loft batting)
Lightweight muslin backing
2 metres/2$\frac{1}{4}$ yards 2.5 cm (1 in)
   wide ribbon
Broderie anglaise (eyelet edging)
Pattern paper

Measuring and cutting out

[1] To make base pattern, set a piece of paper against the base of the basket and draw round. Add 3.5 cm (1$\frac{3}{8}$ in) all round for quilting shrinkage and seam allowance. Cut out.

[2] To make side pattern, measure round the rim, divide this measurement in two and add 6 cm (2$\frac{1}{2}$ in) quilting and seam allowance. Draw a rectangle to equal this measurement in length, times the depth of the basket plus 5 cm (2 in) shrinkage and seam allowance. Cut out half pattern.

[3] Cut out two side sections each in the fabric, wadding (batting) and backing. Cut out base fabric, wadding (batting) and backing.

[4] Cut one piece of broderie anglaise (eyelet edging) that measures twice the circumference of the rim.

Making up

[5] Lay a piece of wadding (batting) over the wrong side of one side section piece and place a piece of backing on top of it. Baste the layers together diagonally and vertically at 7.5 cm (3 in) intervals. Mark up with diagonal quilting lines spaced 2.5 cm (1 in) apart and quilt (see patchwork bedspread with diagonal quilting, steps 8 to 9).

[6] With right sides together and raw edges even join the ends of the quilted side sections together, taking a 1.5 cm ($\frac{5}{8}$ in) seam allowance. Press the seam open.

[7] At the lower edge of the joined side sections sew two lines of gathering stitches either side of the seamline 6 mm ($\frac{1}{4}$ in) apart. With right sides together and raw edges even, set the joined side section piece against the base and draw up the gathering to fit. Stitch all round, taking a 1.5 cm ($\frac{5}{8}$ in) seam allowance. Oversew (*see page 140*) the seam allowances together to neaten. Press.

[8] Neaten (*see page 140*) the top raw edges of the joined side sections. Trim the depth of the basket lining if necessary so that the raw edges come fractionally below the basket rim. Fold 1.5 cm ($\frac{5}{8}$ in) to the wrong side and baste.

[9] Join the ends of the broderie anglaise (eyelet edging) strip to make a circle. Sew one line of gathering stitches 6 mm ($\frac{1}{4}$ in) from the edge. Set the strip against the

back of the basket lining folded edge, adjusting the gathering to fit. Baste, taking a 1 cm ($\frac{3}{8}$ in) seam allowance, attaching two pieces of ribbon, one over the other, at each handle position on the basket, right sides to the outside (fig **14**). On the right side of the basket lining stitch around the top, 6 mm ($\frac{1}{4}$ in) and 1 cm ($\frac{3}{8}$ in) down from the edge.

[10] Place the lining in the basket and tie the ribbons to the handles to finish or slot them through the sides of the basket and tie in a bow.

FABRIC COVERED DIRECTOR'S CHAIR

An existing canvas cover can be overlaid with a more exciting fabric, which used by itself wouldn't be able to stand up to the strain imposed on the seat and back of this type of chair. The chair on page 46 has a seat which is attached to plastic rods that are slotted into a groove cut into each side of the seat frame. The chair back is attached in the same way. It is not difficult to dismantle this chair in order to attach a new cover. If your chair is put together in a different fashion you should still be able to remove the seat and back frames. You can then cover the seat and back fabric sections in the same way that they were made. You should only attempt this treatment if the existing cover is in reasonably good condition and isn't too badly stretched.

You will need
Mediumweight cotton fabric

Measuring and cutting out

[1] Unslot the chair seat and unpick the stitching forming the rod channel at each side of the canvas. Mea-

sure the width of the seat fabric from raw edge to raw edge. Next measure the seat from front to back and add 15 cm (6 in) all round for hems. Cut a piece of fabric to these dimensions. Repeat for the chair back.

Making up

[2] Trim away the hem allowance at the back and front of the canvas seat to remove bulk. Lay the canvas right side down on top of the wrong side of the seat fabric and pin together at intervals across the surface, making sure that the two fabrics are flat.

[3] Wrap the fabric over the canvas at the front and back edges, folding a double hem. Pin in position. At each side of the seat at the back and front, trim away 3 cm (1$\frac{1}{4}$ in) of the hem allowance as shown in fig **15**. Stitch across the seat along the back and front edges close to the inner folded edge of the hem.

[4] Fold back the sides of the seat over the canvas along the original foldlines and stitch from front to back at the required distance from each fold to make a snug casing for the rod (fig **16**). Slot the rods through the seat sides and replace in the grooves.

[5] Repeat this covering procedure for the chair back, marking the position of each side screw on the outer edge of the fabric. When you replace the chair back, pierce the fabric carefully and screw the back into position.

FABRIC COVERED DECKCHAIR

The covering of the existing deckchair canvas with a different fabric employs the same method as is used to cover the director's chair above.

You will need
Mediumweight cotton fabric
Tacks

Measuring and cutting out

[1] Pull out the tacks that hold the canvas in place at each end of the deckchair frame, using a chisel and

Fig 13

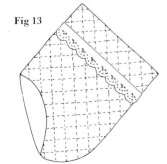

Fig 14

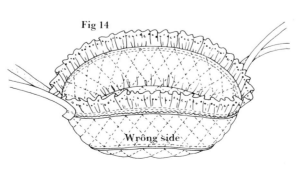

Wrong side

Fig 15

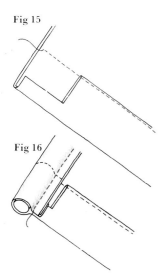

Fig 16

Fig 17

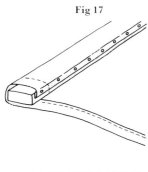

Fig 18

hammer, gently levering the chisel head between tack head and canvas. Take the length and width measurements of the canvas, adding 7.5 cm (3 in) hem allowance to each long side. Cut one piece of fabric to these dimensions.

Making up

2 Trim away the hem allowance down the long sides of the deckchair if there is any, to reduce bulk. Lay the canvas face downwards centrally on top of the wrong side of the fabric. Turn in a double hem allowance down each long side. Pin. Stitch close to the inner folded edge down both sides of the cover.

3 Remove the wooden bars from the top and bottom of the deckchair. Place the top bar on the canvas and fold over the fabric along the original foldline, folding under a seam allowance at the raw edge to neaten as before (fig **17**). Hammer a tack into the centre of the bar through the cover to secure in place. Keeping the cover at right angles to the bar with the foldline running evenly along it, hammer tacks home at 5 cm (2 in) intervals along the length of the bar.

4 Repeat step 3 for the bottom of the cover, which is usually rolled on to a round piece of wood. Replace the wooden bars.

SMOCKED STOOL COVER

You will need

Fabric
Cushion pad for the stool top
Smocked heading tape of the desired depth
Tape for ties

Measuring and cutting out

1 Attach the cushion pad to each stool leg with tapes which have been stitched on to the side of the cushion at the points nearest the legs of the stool.

2 Measure the diameter of the cushion pad, A–B, its circumference B–B, and the length from the top of the pad to the ground C–D (fig **18**). Cut a pattern for the top of the pad following the instructions given for the round cushion cover on page 118, step 2, adding a seam allowance of 2.5 cm (1 in) all round.

3 To calculate the width required for the skirt multiply the circumference of the cushion pad by two (or whatever multiple is required by the maker of the heading tape, as fullness requirements can vary) and add 3 cm (1¼ in) for seams. You will need a length of heading tape equal to this width plus an allowance for neatening the ends.

4 To calculate the length take the measurement C–D and add 2.5 cm (1 in) for the top seam allowance and 5 cm (2 in) for a double hem at the base.

5 The skirt will probably be wider than your fabric width. Cut two sections of the required length that will make up the width when joined down the long edges. Allow extra fabric for matching patterns across seams (*see page 95, step 8*).

Making up

6 Right sides together, raw edges even, join skirt sections down the length to make a circle, taking a 1.5 cm (⅝ in) seam allowance. Press seams open. Turn 2.5 cm (1 in) to the wrong side at top edge and press.

7 Attach the smocked heading tape following the maker's instructions and the explanations on page 94, setting the tape 3 mm (⅛ in) from the top foldline.

8 Pull up the skirt to the required circumference, knotting the tape cords but not cutting them.

9 Place the cushion top section inside the skirt, the right side of the top against the wrong side of the skirt, the top raw edges even with the folded edge of the skirt. Pin all round, adjusting gathers if necessary, then baste. Stitch along skirt top following top line of stitching on the heading tape. The cover forms a 'hat' shape.

10 Set the cover over the stool and check the length. Remove. Turn 2.5 cm (1 in) to the wrong side twice at the base edge to make a double hem. Press. Hem by hand or machine stitch close to the inner folded edge.

DROP-IN CHAIR SEAT COVER WITH DOUBLE PIPING AND BOX EDGED SIDES

You will need

Fabric for the seat top, sides and bias strips
Heavyweight fabric for lining the underneath of the chair seat

Pre-shrunk piping cord
Tacks
Wadding (batting) (optional)

Measuring and cutting out

1 Measure across the seat top both ways (fig **19**); this means the part of the seat that is visible when it is dropped in place in the chair frame. Cut a piece of fabric to these dimensions plus 2 cm (¾ in) all round.

2 Remove the seat from the chair. Carefully remove the existing tacks holding the bottom lining and cover in place, using a chisel held parallel with the frame and positioned just under the head of each tack. Tap the chisel sharply with a hammer, levering with the chisel to push up the tack head, then pull out with pliers. Discard the used tacks.

3 There should be a calico (muslin) covering on the top of the chair seat. If there is a layer of wadding (batting) above it, remove this and replace with fresh wadding (batting) cut to the same size.

4 Cut out enough bias strips (*see page 140*) for the covered piping to go twice round the chair seat when joined.

5 For the chair seat sides cut one piece of fabric that measures 20 cm (8 in) wide by the length of the four sides plus 10 cm (4 in).

6 Measure the underneath of the chair seat from frame edge to frame edge and cut one piece of fabric to these dimensions plus 1 cm (⅜ in) all round.

Fig 19

Making up

7 Make up two strips of covered piping (*see page 141*) each long enough to go round the chair cover, 2 cm ($\frac{3}{4}$ in) in from the edge. Pin and baste the first length of piping to the edges of the cover piece, lining up the piping stitching line with the cover seamline. Begin and end the piping at the back of the cover, making a neat join (*see page 141*). Using the zipper foot on your machine stitch all round. Clip the piping seam allowance at the corners to ease. Attach the second length of piping directly over the first, stitching along the first stitching line (fig **20**).

8 Fold 2.5 cm (1 in) to the wrong side at one end of the side strip. Beginning midway along the back edge, with right side of the strip against the piping, pin the strip all the way round the cover along the piping stitching lines taking a 1.5 cm ($\frac{5}{8}$ in) seam allowance

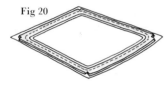

Fig 20

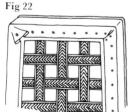

Fig 21

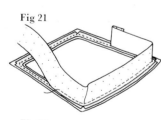

Fig 22

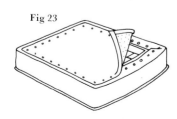

Fig 23

(fig **21**). Overlap the folded portion of the strip by 2.5 cm (1 in) when you reach the starting point at the back. Trim the excess fabric at the strip end.

9 Clip the corners of the strip seam allowance to ease. Trim the seam allowances of the piping to 1 cm ($\frac{3}{8}$ in) and 12 mm ($\frac{1}{2}$ in) respectively to grade the seam allowance thicknesses. Press all the allowances towards the side strip.

10 Turn the cover to the right side and set it upside down in front of you. If there is any, set the new wadding (batting) in place furry side down, followed by the existing pad and its frame, again upside down, inside the box shaped cover.

11 Keeping the piping level with the seat top edge, wrap the back section of fabric over the frame base and attach it temporarily with tacks set half way into the wood, starting at the centre and working outwards, placing tacks at about 2.5 cm (1 in) intervals. Lift the front of the frame so that it rests on its back edge and pull the fabric tautly into position over the front edge. Tack as before, checking the piping is lying level with the top edge. Repeat this operation on the remaining sides.

12 Pull up the fabric hard over each corner and tack it temporarily in place (fig **22**). Repeat this procedure for the other three corners. At each corner, fold the excess fabric towards the centre of each side of the frame and tack flat to neaten.

13 Check the top of the cover to make sure that the fabric lies evenly taut. Lift tacks a few at a time and reposition if you are not satisfied, then hammer the tacks home all round the frame.

14 Set the lining fabric against the seat base. Turning under 2 cm ($\frac{3}{4}$ in) along all edges, tack close to the fold at intervals of 2.5 cm (1 in), making sure the fabric is pulled taut and that it covers the first set of tacks (fig **23**).

RE-COVERING WOODEN HEADBOARDS AND FOOTBOARDS

You will need
Fabric
Gimp or flat braid for edging, as old measurements plus 20 cm (8 in)
Matching gimp pins (small headed tacks)
Round headed pins
Tacks
Clear adhesive
Pattern paper

Measuring and cutting out

1 Remove the existing gimp or braid carefully and make a note of each length. Remove the fabric from each side of the two boards following the previous instructions, step 2. Mark each piece 'front head', 'back head' and so on. Lay each section flat on the floor and calculate the amount of fabric needed. Add seam allowances of 2 cm ($\frac{3}{4}$ in) all round. If the fabric panels are wider than the width of your fabric, position a width of fabric at the centre of the bed with narrow strips set to each side. Allow extra fabric for matching patterns across seams (*see page 95, step 8*).

2 Using the old fabric pieces as your pattern, lay each piece with the right side uppermost on the right side of the fabric, the edges folded in along the original foldlines. Pin flat in position. Cut round each piece, adding 2 cm ($\frac{3}{4}$ in) seam allowance all round. Unpin the new front headboard piece and mark a chalk line down the centre on the wrong side. Mark a corresponding chalk line on the headboard.

3 Set the headboard fabric right side uppermost against the bed headboard, matching chalk lines. Pin from top to bottom of the chalk line to attach, the fabric overlapping the surround evenly. Place a tack half way in at the top and bottom, just inside the line to which the old covering extended. Then, smoothing the fabric taut, set it in position all the way round, placing tacks temporarily half way into the wood at 2.5 cm (1 in) intervals (fig **24**).

4 Remove the pins and adjust the fabric if need be, removing tacks a few at a time and re-smoothing until you are satisfied. Hammer each tack into the wooden surround, being very careful not to harm the wood.

5 Trim the fabric all the way round to the outside edges of the tack heads. Place a new length of gimp or flat braid over the tacked raw edges of the covering, butting it up to the show-wood line so that no raw edges or tacks can be seen. Set it in position using a small amount of clear adhesive, matching gimp pins or small headed tacks if you prefer. Do not use much adhesive or it will discolour the trimming. Fold the trimming into a mitre at each corner and secure it with a gimp pin (tack). Tuck under the end to the wrong side and secure with a gimp pin to finish.

6 Repeat this operation for the front footboard of the bed, then repeat for the backs of the boards, omitting the pinning stage unless the boards are padded.

Fig 24

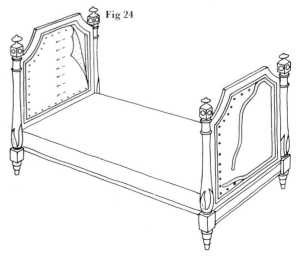

NAPKINS

The napkins on page 45 are 60 cm (24 in) square, which means you can cut two from a 67 cm (26½ in) length of 137 cm (54 in) wide fabric.

You will need
Fabric
Matching or contrasting thread
 for topstitching

Making up

☐1 Cut out the number of napkins required, adding a hem allowance of 3 cm (1¼ in) all round.

☐2 Fold 1.5 cm (⅝ in) to the wrong side twice along the edge of each napkin, mitring the corners (*see page 141*). Press. Slipstitch (*see page 140*) across the mitre.

☐3 Stitch around each napkin to finish, close to the inner folded edge (fig **25**).

POLE END COVER

This pole end cover consists of two circles of fabric, one print and one lining, which are stitched together and gathered up over a pole end so that it blends in with the curtains.

You will need
Fabric
Lining
Length of string
Pencil
Pattern paper

Measuring and cutting out

☐1 Measure from the centre top of the pole end to the neck and add 5 cm (2 in) ruffle/seam allowance. This measurement is the radius of the fabric circles you are going to cut out.

☐2 Fold a piece of paper wider and longer than twice the radius, in half. Tie the length of string to the

Fig 25

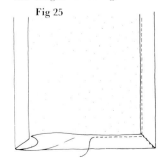

pencil and cut it so that it equals the radius. Pin the string into the fold of the paper halfway down its length. Holding the pencil upright, draw a half circle from folded edge to folded edge. Cut round the pencil outline and unfold the pattern.

Making up

☐3 Using the pattern, cut out one piece of fabric and one piece of lining. Set one over the other, right sides together. Stitch all round, taking a 1 cm (⅜ in) seam allowance and leaving a gap of 10 cm (4 in) through which to turn. Clip curve.

☐4 Turn and press. Turn in the opening edges in line with the remainder of the seam and slipstitch (*see page 140*) to close. Run two lines of gathering stitches around the edge of the circle 4 cm (1½ in) and 3 cm (1¼ in) in from the edge (fig **26**).

☐5 Pull up the gathers slightly then set over the pole end. Draw up the gathers tightly and wrap the threads around the pole and tie to secure.

POLE COVER

You will need
Fabric
Matching thread

Measuring and cutting out

☐1 Cut 1 piece of fabric (joined if necessary) to equal twice the length of the pole plus 5 cm (2 in) for seams, by the circumference of the pole plus 4.5 cm (1¾ in) for seam allowances and ease, plus 10 cm (4 in) for double ruffle at top and bottom.

Making up

☐2 Follow steps 2 to 5 of ruffled casing for metal arm (*see page 106*), leaving both short ends of the tube open and neatening as in step 3. Allow double ruffles of 2.5 cm (1 in) at top and bottom of the tube.

Fig 26

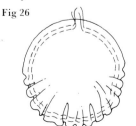

SEWING TECHNIQUES

TEN USEFUL STITCHES

BASTING/TACKING (fig **1**)

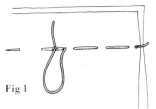

Fig 1

A long running stitch, basting can be worked quickly by machine or by hand and holds two or more pieces of fabric in position ready for final stitching. Begin hand basting with a knot so that stitches are easy to remove. Simply cut off the knot and pull the thread through the fabric from the other end.

BUTTONHOLE STITCH (fig **2**)

Fig 2

This is used for neatening buttonholes and for stitching hooks and eyes and press fasteners firmly in place. Insert the needle upward through the fabric at the desired distance from the edge and twist the working thread around the point. Pull the needle through, bringing the knot you have formed to the edge.

HEMMING STITCH (fig **3**)

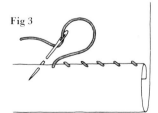

Fig 3

This is used to attach a folded hem edge to flat fabric. Fasten the working thread inside the hem, then make small even slanting stitches through the fabric and hem in one movement. Pick up only one or two threads of fabric with each stitch.

HERRINGBONE (CATCH) STITCH (fig **4**)

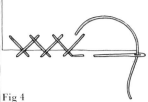

Fig 4

This is used to hold single hems firmly in place. Work from left to right with the folded hem edge facing towards you. Fasten the working thread and bring it up through the hem near the edge. Move about 6 mm (¼ in) diagonally to the right across the hem edge and take a small stitch from right to left just above the hem edge. Stitch across the hem edge 6 mm (¼ in) diagonally to the right and take a small stitch diagonally to the left. Bring the thread diagonally to the right again and take another small stitch to the left just above the hem edge. Continue along the hem.

This stitch is used to join wadding (batting) edges together. The stitches can be large and loose, catching only one or two fabric threads.

LADDERSTITCH (fig **5**)

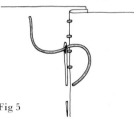

Fig 5

When joining patterned fabric the pattern must be matched across seams by tacking the fabric pieces together from the right side.

Press under the seam allowance along one fabric edge and place over the flat seam allowance of the other so that the pattern matches exactly. Pin.

Insert needle into the folded edge between the two layers of fabric and bring it out again 2 cm (¾ in) along the fold. Take a small stitch directly across the join and take another 2 cm (¾ in) down the fabric along the seamline. Take a small stitch directly across into the fold again and take another 2 cm ($\frac{3}{4}$ in) stitch. Repeat along the seam, forming ladder-like stitches.

When the seam is completed the two pieces of fabric can be folded with right sides together ready for stitching.

LOCKSTITCH (fig 6)

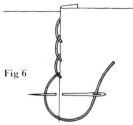

Fig 6

Used in curtain making to hold lining and interlining loosely against the wrong side of the curtain fabric. Fold the lining / interlining back against the pins (see Curtains, page 98). Stitch from top to bottom. Take a stitch through the folded edge and curtain fabric at right angles to the folded edge, picking up only one or two threads of fabric with each stitch. Make the next stitch about 5 cm (2 in) to the right, taking the thread over the needle to produce a loop.

OVERSEWING (fig 7)

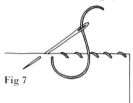

Fig 7

This is also called overcasting and is used to neaten raw edges. Working from left to right take thread diagonally over the fabric edge, making small even stitches and bringing the needle through the fabric about 3 mm ($\frac{1}{8}$ in) from the edge.

PRICKSTITCH (fig 8)

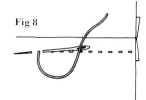

Fig 8

Also called stabstitch, this makes a unobtrusive stitching line. Bring the needle through to the upper side of the fabric. Insert the needle just behind where the thread came out, then take a stitch about 6 mm ($\frac{1}{4}$ in) in front of that point. Bring the needle through to the upper side and repeat.

RUNNING (GATHERING) STITCH (fig 9)

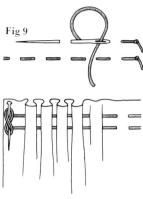

Fig 9

This stitch is used mainly for gathering. Secure the thread, then make small evenly spaced stitches along the fabric. Finish with another backstitch. When used for gathering work two rows either side of the seamline 6 mm ($\frac{1}{4}$ in) apart, leaving the threads dangling at one end. To gather, pull on the threads gently and slide the fabric along. Secure the threads by twisting in a figure eight around a pin.

SLIPSTITCH (fig 10)

Used to attach a folded edge to a flat edge as in hemming or to join two folded edges together.

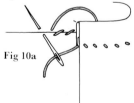

Fig 10a

Hemming: (fig **10a**) working from right to left with the inner folded hem edge towards you, take a tiny stitch into the main fabric close to the folded edge. Without pulling the thread through, slip the needle into the folded edge as close as possible to the first stitch and bring it out about 6 mm ($\frac{1}{4}$ in) to the left. Pull the thread through and take another small stitch into the main fabric.

Joining folded edges: (fig **10b**)

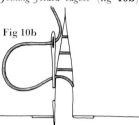

Fig 10b

fasten the thread inside one folded edge and then cross over the opening into the opposite fold. Make a stitch about 6 mm ($\frac{1}{4}$ in) long and pull the needle through the other fold again. Repeat, working backwards and forwards across the gap and inserting the needle slightly to the inside of the fold. The stitches will be invisible.

TWO USEFUL SEAMS

FLAT FELL SEAM (fig 11)

This seam is very strong and used on furnishings frequently

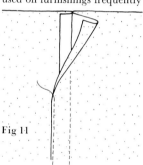

Fig 11

washed, such as tablecloths.

Place the two fabric pieces with right sides together and matching raw edges and stitch as for a plain seam. Press the seam allowances to one side and then trim the underneath allowance to 6 mm ($\frac{1}{4}$ in). Wrap the top seam allowance over the trimmed one to enclose its raw edge, folding 6 mm ($\frac{1}{4}$ in) under. Press flat and stitch along the folded edge.

FRENCH SEAM (fig 12)

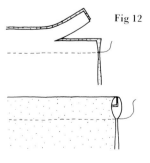

Fig 12

Another self-neatening seam used mainly on lightweight fabrics, it can only be used on straight grain fabric edges.

Join the two fabric pieces with wrong sides together, matching raw edges, taking a 6 mm ($\frac{1}{4}$ in) seam allowance. Refold the fabric with right sides together and stitch the seam again 1 cm ($\frac{3}{8}$ in) from the first stitching line to enclose the raw edges. Press.

BIAS STRIPS AND PIPING

BIAS STRIPS

These are used for covering piping cord and for binding raw edges smoothly.

1 Find the bias of your fabric and fold over the selvedge so that it lies parallel to the weft (the cross threads of the fabric). Cut along the fold and use this edge for cutting bias strips (fig **13**).

2 Mark the strips in tailor's chalk parallel to the bias edge, using a ruler made from card to the desired strip width. If cutting strips for covering piping cord, cut them to give a 1.5 cm ($\frac{5}{8}$ in) seam allowance when wrapped around the cord. Double the seam allowance of 1.5 cm ($\frac{5}{8}$ in) and add the circumference of the cord.

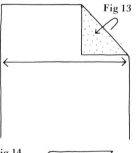

Fig 13

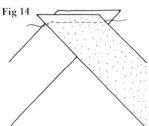

Fig 14

3 To join bias strips match the ends as shown (fig **14**), right sides together. Stitch across the join, taking a 6 mm ($\frac{1}{4}$ in) seam allowance. Press the seam open.

PIPING

Piping is a strip of bias cut fabric inserted into the seams of furnishings to give them a tailored and professional finish. It also strengthens seams. It can either be flat or corded. In corded piping the bias strip is folded in half around a length of piping cord. This can be bought in various thicknesses ranging from 00 to 6. Number 3 is the most commonly used. The cord should always be shrunk before it is used, otherwise the finished piping could pucker badly when the home furnishing is washed.

If a length of piping goes all the way round an object the ends must be joined. Allow an extra 5 cm (2 in) for the join. The cord can also be joined by unravelling each end, cutting each strand of cord in a different place and intertwining them (fig **15**). The ends are then whipped around with sewing thread

Fig 15

Fig 16

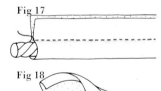

Fig 17

Fig 18

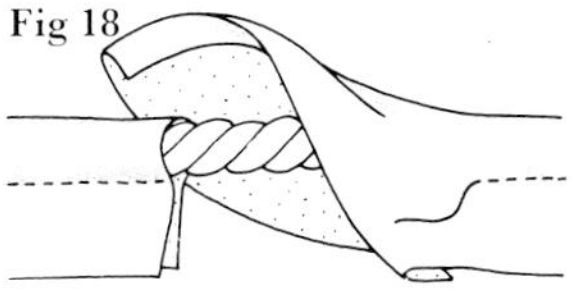

and stitched through with the same thread (fig **16**).

1 To cover piping cord, fold the bias strip around the cord right side out, raw edges matching. Pin and stitch close to the cord, using the zipper foot (fig **17**).

2 To join covered piping, unpick the last 2.5 cm (1 in) at one end. Turn under 12 mm ($\frac{1}{2}$ in) of the fabric to conceal the raw edge. Cut off the last 2.5 cm (1 in) of the cord. Insert the other end of the covered piping so the cord ends meet and the other raw edge is enclosed (fig **18**). Stitch across the join along seamline.

MITRED CORNER

FOLDING A MITRE, SINGLE HEM

1 Turn under the two sides for the desired amount and press. Mark each raw edge where the turnings intersect with a pin (fig **19**).

2 Unfold the turnings and press in the corner at an angle from pin to pin (fig **20**).

3 Refold the turnings so that the corner folds

Fig 19

Fig 20

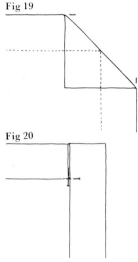

into a neat mitre and slipstitch its edges together. Press.

Fig 21

Fig 22

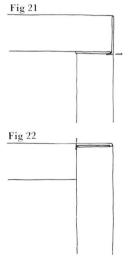

FOLDING A MITRE, DOUBLE HEM

1 Turn under the sides once and press. Double the turning along one side and mark where it falls on the other side edge with a pin (fig **21**). Unfold the turning to single width again.

2 Double the turning along the other side and mark where it falls on the other side edge with a pin (fig **22**). Unfold to single width.

3 Press in the corner at an angle from pin to pin as in fig **20** above but with single width hems folded in. Double the turnings and the corner will fold into a neat mitre. Slipstitch its edges together.

TRIMMING A MITRED CORNER

1 Follow steps 1 and 2 of folding a mitred corner in a single hem. Then trim the corner to within 6 mm ($\frac{1}{4}$ in) of the diagonal fold. Turn in 6 mm ($\frac{1}{4}$ in) across the corner.

2 If you want neatened hem edges, fold them under by 6 mm ($\frac{1}{4}$ in) and press. Fold in the hem along the original foldlines to make a mitred corner. Slipstitch its edges together. Hem by hand or stitch along the inner folded edges to secure.

FASTENINGS

CENTRED ZIP (ZIPPER)

1 Measure the length of the zip (zipper) and mark its length on the seamline. Stitch a simple seam to its

Fig 23

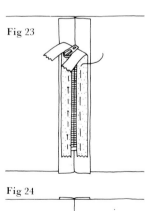

Fig 24

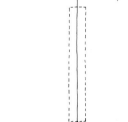

base point and then reverse to secure the stitching. Change the stitch length on the machine to a long one and baste the opening. Reverse the stitching at the top of the opening and continue stitching the seam with a normal length stitch. Press the seam open.

2 Place the zip (zipper) face down over the seam allowances with the teeth centred exactly over the seamline. Pin and baste in position through all layers 6 mm ($\frac{1}{4}$ in) to either side of the teeth (fig **23**).

3 Turn to the right side. Using the zipper foot, topstitch the zip (zipper) in place just inside the basting lines, pivoting at the corners (fig **24**). Alternatively, hand stitch, using prickstitch.

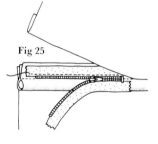

Fig 25

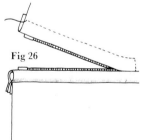

Fig 26

PIPED SEAM ZIP (ZIPPER)

1 Pipe one edge of seam. Do not close opening.

2 Open the zip (zipper) and place right side downwards on the piped seam, teeth against piping stitching line. Baste. Stitch close to the teeth, using zipper foot (fig **25**).

3 Turn back seam allowance to wrong side so piping lies at opening edge. Close the zip (zipper). Press under seam allowance at the other side of the opening. Bring folded edge over the zip (zipper) to meet piping. Baste seam. Stitch 6 mm ($\frac{1}{4}$ in) from folded edge and across zip ends to piping edge (fig **26**).

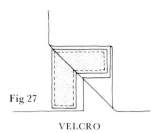

Fig 27

Fig 29

Fig 31

A B   A B   A B   A B

VELCRO

This fastener consists of two strips of material, one covered in loops and the other with small hooks which cling together when pressed. It is available in various widths and colour. Make sure you choose the right weight for the job. You will have to allow greater seam allowances if you are applying Velcro wider than 1 cm ($\frac{3}{8}$ in).

Fig 28

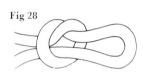

1. Pin and baste the tape in place down the long edges either side of the opening. Stitch, using a zipper foot on the machine (fig 27).

SLIP KNOT

1. Hold the two twine ends in one hand. Put the right end over the left and bring it back over the left end again. Pull the right end up through the loop that has formed. Pull to tighten (fig 28).

RUFFLES

The fullness of a ruffle can vary between one and a half to three times the length of the edge to which it is to be attached, depending on the fabric weight and the desired effect.

SINGLE RUFFLE

1. Decide on the finished depth of the ruffle. Add a

Fig 30

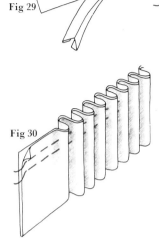

1.5 cm ($\frac{5}{8}$ in) seam allowance and a double hem allowance of 1 cm to 2 cm ($\frac{3}{8}$ in to $\frac{3}{4}$ in).

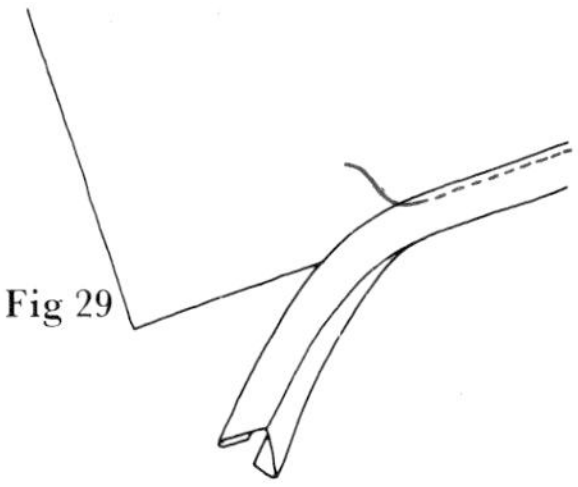

2. Join the ends of the ruffle strips together with flat fell seams to make a continuous or longer length. If the ruffle is not continuous make a double turning of 6 mm ($\frac{1}{4}$ in) at each end and stitch.

3. Turn up a double hem along the lower edge of the ruffle and stitch.

4. Gather up the raw edge to required size. For long ruffles divide the ruffle and the edge to which it is to be attached into an equal number of sections. Work two rows of gathering stitches in each ruffle section. With right sides together, raw edges even and matching section dividing points, gather up the ruffle to fit the main fabric edge. Pin, baste and stitch together. Neaten the seam with machine zigzagging and press upwards.

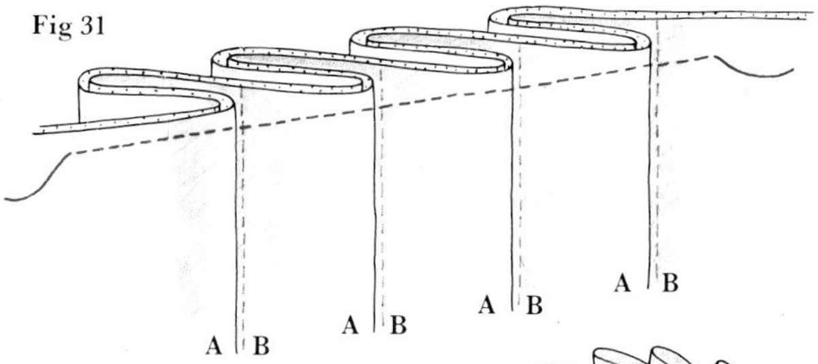

5. The ruffle edge can also be bound with contrasting bias strips before gathering. Either turn in the long edge of the bias strip to neaten and fold it over the ruffle edge and topstitch in place (fig 29) or seam it to the edge with right sides together, raw edges even. Turn it over the edge and hem in place on the wrong side. You do not need a hem allowance if you are binding a ruffle.

DOUBLE RUFFLE

1. Cut double the required depth plus twice the top seam allowance. Join the ends together with plain seams.

2. Fold the ruffle in half, matching raw edges and wrong sides, and gather the top edges in the same way as for a single ruffle (fig 30).

KNIFE PLEAT RUFFLE

This is a variation on a double ruffle and is usually applied to cushions or curtain edgings.

1. Decide on an appropriate pleat width. Next divide the edge to which the pleats are to be attached by the width of pleat; this will give you the number of pleats for the edge. Multiply this number by three to get the

Fig 32

width of fabric needed for making up the pleated section and add allowances for seams and side hems, if any.

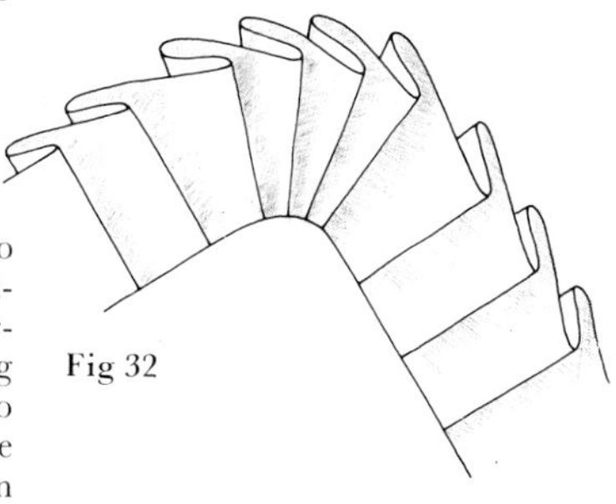

2. Cut out and make up the complete pleat strip in the same way as for a double ruffle.

3. Mark the positioning lines for each pleat on the fabric edge. Mark the pleat line A first, and then measure twice the pleat width from this line and mark the placement line B. Leave a pleat width gap and return to the beginning of the sequence, repeating until the end of the section is reached.

4. To pleat up, fold the fabric on the first pleat line and bring it to the next placement line. Pin. Repeat until all the fabric has been pleated (fig 31). Baste along the top of the pleats and stitch in place as needed. If you are attaching a pleated ruffle to a cushion you will find it necessary to make slightly smaller pleats at each corner with the base of each pleat overlapping (fig 32).

INDEX

Algonquin Hotel, New York, 73
Arts and Crafts Movement, The, 6, 20, 42, 78
Ascot Box, 70, 72
Austrian blinds, *see* Blinds

Baker, Olive, 6
Baskets
  Moses, quilted, with matching coverlet, 86, *87*, 134–6
  with quilted lining, 86, 87, 136
Basting, 139
Bathroom, (Bucks), 33–4
  London house, 84
Bauhaus (print), 78, *78*, 82, 83
Bay window, swags and tails, *59*, 60, 102
Bedcovers, *see* Bedspreads and Valances
Bedroom
  attic, London, 92
  boy's, 82–3
  Chinese style, 90–91
  Farmhouse, 16, 62, 64
  Sweet Pea print, 26, 28
Bedspreads, 125–132
  fitted and piped, with pillow gusset and kick pleats, 55, 56, 125–6
  fitted, quilted, with contrast piping, *73*, 74, 130–131
  lined, 18, *18*, 26, 68, 125
  fitted, with pillow gussets and scalloped edge, 28, 126–7
  with quilted dragon panels, 91, *91*, 131–2
  patchwork, 30, 64, 128–9
  with diagonal quilting, 31, 127–8
Bias strips, 140
Bladon (print), 34, *34*, 70, 72
Blinds, 109–113
  Austrian, lined, with ruffle, 9, *9*, 10, 112
  unlined, with double ruffle, *23*, 24, *24*, 55, *55*, 56, *56*, 111–2
  roller, 84, 92, 112–3
  Roman, 34, 52, 83, *83*, 109–111
Briarwood (print), 28
Bungalow, Mesnil-le-Roi, 20–21
Burnham (print), 52
Butterfield, Lindsay, P, 7
Buttonhole, 139

Capriccio (print), 9, *10*, *23*, 24, 46, 72
Ceiling, tented, gathered, 72, 132–3
Chelsea Arts Club, 51, 55
  Bedroom, 55–6
  Club room, 51–52

founders, 51
Churchill, Sir Winston, 76
Clandon (print), 76, 77
Clementina (print), 38
Collections, fabric
  Chesham
    Bauhaus, 78, *78*, 82, 83
    Ianthe, 42, *42*
    Kasak, 82, 83, 84, *85*
    Lodden, 21
    Melrose, 80, 81, *81*
    Tambourine, 49
    Zebak, *51*, 52, *52*, 66, 67, 68, *68*
  Chesham II
    Clandon, 76, *76*, 77
    Clementina, 38
    Hedgerow, 24, 48, *49*
    Hermia, 64
    Melbury, 60
    Petronella, 62, 74, *75*
    Salazar, *36*, 38
    Scherzo, 68
    Trent, 10
  Cotton
    Briarwood, 28
    Hera, 42
    Honeysuckle, 21
    Penelope, 12
    Sweet Pea, 26, *26*, 28, *28*, 55, *55*
    Terrace, 74
    Willow, 56, 92, *92*
  East India, 9, 90
    Bladon, 34, *34*, 70, 72
    Capriccio, 9, 10, *10*, 23, 24, *24*, 46, 70, 72
    Keswick, 18
    Madison, 9, 10, *10*
    Mariana, 34
    Opium, 30, 31, 80, 90, 91
    Santana, 14, 44, 46
    Suki, *58*, 59, *59*, 60, 80, 90, 91
    Tana lawns, 26, 30, 31, 62, *62*, 86
    Classic, 86, 87
    Mayfair, 70, 72, *72*
  Union
    Burnham, 52
Collier, Susan, 26, 30
Cornices, *see* Pelmets
Covers, bed, *see* Bedspreads and Valances
Covers, cushion, *see* Cushions
Covers, seat
  chair seat, drop-in, with double piping and boxed sides, 42, 137–8
  deck chair, fabric covered, 48, 49, *49*, 136–7
  director's chair, fabric covered, 46, *47*, 136
  sofa, scroll armed, loose, with piping and kick pleated skirt, 10, 113–6
  stool, smocked, 77, 137
Curtains, 94–104
  cased headings, 99

combined curtain and valance, 34, *34*, 100
curved valance and ruffled piped edge, 100–102
cutting out, 95–6
fixed, *55*, 56, 99
  with contrast bound heading, 99–100
headings, 94
interlined, with triple pinch pleat headings, 60, 88, *89*, 98–9
jabots, *see* Swags and Tails
linings and stiffenings, 95
measuring for, 95
quick casing for lightweight kitchen/bathroom curtain, 99
ruffled, with sewn-in lining and contrast piping, 14, 74, 97
stiffenings and linings, 95
swag and contrast lined tails (jabots), 88, 104
swags and tails (jabots) for bay window, 60, 102–4
track poles and accessories, 94–5
unlined, 96–7
with cartridge pleat heading, *9*, 10, 18, 21, 52, 64, 74, 96
with locked-in lining, 10, 18, 21, 52, 64, 72, 74, 77, 81, 97–8
with pinch pleat heading, 64, 81, 96
with smocked heading, 77, 96
with triple pinch pleat heading, 72, 96
Cushions, 117–122
  attaching to chair with ties, 121
  box edged, covers, 119–120
    vinyl coated, 36
  bunk cover, 38, 122
  buttoned lounger, 48, 49, 121–2
  heart-shaped, with double ruffle and piping, 91, 119
  knife edged covers, 117
  pad, 120–121
  rectangular, box edged, cover, with piping, 21, 38, 52, 119–120
    boxed edged, with piping, 52, 119
    cover, with side opening, 117–8
  round, box edged, cover with piping, 10, 81, 119, 120, 141
    cover, with back zip opening, 118–9
    cover, with double ruffle, 10, 142
    cover, with hand sewn

side opening, 118, 142
  with contrast piping, 81, 120, 141
shaping, to fit chair seat, 120–121
square, cover, 79, 117
  cover, with double ruffle, 10, 117, 142
  cover, with piping, 72, 83, 117, 142
  cover, with side opening, 117–8
  patchwork, 64, 128
  with knife-pleated ruffle, 28, 118, 142
  with piping, 68, 72, 117, 142
Cuzner, Bernard, 6

Deck chair, fabric covered, 48, 49, *49*, 136
De Morgan, William, 7
Delaunay, Sonia, 7, 82
Designers, 6, 7, 9, 20, 25, 66, 78
Director's chair, fabric covered, 46, *47*, 136
Doran, J M, 7
Dorrell, William Haynes, 62
Dresser, Dr Christopher, 6, 40

East India Collection, *see* Collections
East India House, 6, 9
Edwardian house, London, 9–10

Farmhouse, Morecambe Bay, 12–15
  Sevenoaks, 30–32
Fastenings, 141
Footboards, recovering, 26, 28, 136
Freud, Clement, MP, 70

Gathering stitch, 140
Goad, Valerie, 26, 30

Haward, David, 58
Haward, Sidney, 7, 26, 55, 58, *64*
Headboards, recovering, 26, 28, 138
Hedgerow (print), 24, 48, *49*
Hemming, 139
Hera (print), 42
Hermia (print), 64
Honeysuckle (print), 21
Hoshi (Edwardian schooner), 36, 38, *38*
Hotel, Ashford, Kent
  conservatory, 44, 46
  garden, 48–9
House, Eaton Terrace, 88
  Strawberry Hill, 58, 60

Ianthe (print), 42, *42*

Kasak (print), 82, 83, 84, *85*
Kempston, James and Ingrid, 44
Keswick (print), 18
King, Jessie, 6
Kitchen, terraced cottage, London, 78
town house, London, 23–4
Knox, Archibald, 6

Ladderstitch, 139–140
Laflin, John, 7, 9, 25, 66
Liberty, Arthur, 6, 20
Liberty Guild, 42
Littler, Edmund, 6
Lockstitch, 140
Lodden (print), 21
Loose covers, *see* Covers and Cushions

MacCaw, Sandy, 23
Madison (print), 9, 10, *10*, *17*, 18
Manor house, Kent, 17–18
Mariana (print), 34
Mawson, Sidney, 7
Melbury (print), 60
Melrose (print), 80, *81*
Miles, Frank, 7
Mitred corner, 141
Morris, William, 6, 10, 20, 28, 40, *41*, 42, 56
Moses basket (bassinet), 87, *87*, 134–6

Napkins, 44, 46, 139
Napper, Harry, 7
Nevill, Bernard, 7

Office, farmhouse, 80
Opium (print), 31, 90, 91
Oversewing, 140

Paterson, Edgar, 7
Paul, William, 7
Pauwels, Madame, 20, 21
Pearson, John, 6
Peduzzi, Richard, 7
Pelmets (cornices), 105–6
cornice board, 105
piped, with lined contrast-edged ruffle, 14, 74, 106
with piping and double ruffle, 81, 105–6
Penelope (print), 12, 14, *14*

Petronella (print), 62, 74, *75*
Piping, 141
Pole, cover, 55, 56, 139
end cover, 139
Prickstitch, 140
Prints
Bauhaus, 78, *78*, 82, 83
Bladon, 34, *34*, 70, 72
Briarwood, 28
Burnham, 52
Capriccio, 9, *10*, 23, 24, *24*, 46, 70, 72
Clandon, 76, *76*, 77
Clementina, 38
Hedgerow, 24, 48, *49*
Hera, 42
Hermia, 64
Honeysuckle, 21
Grey chintz, 88
Ianthe, 42, *42*
Kasak, 82, 83, 84, *85*
Keswick, 18
Lodden, 21
Madison, 9, 10, *10*, 17, 18, *18*
Mariana, 34
Mayfair, 72
Melbury, 60
Melrose, 80, 81, *81*
Morris, William, 20, *21*, *41*, 42, 56
Opium, 31, 80, 90, 91
Penelope, 12, 14, *14*
Petronella, 62, *62*, 74, *75*
Salazar, *36*, 38
Santana, 14, 44, 46
Scherzo, 63, 68
Suki, 58, *58*, 59, *59*, 60, 80, 90, 91
Sweet Pea, 26, *26*, 28, *28*, 55, *55*
Tambourine, 49
Tana lawns, 26, 30, *31*, 62, *62*, 70, 72, *72*, 86, 87
Terrace, 74
Trent, 10
Willow, 56, 92, *92*
Zebak, 51, *51*, 52, *52*, 66, *67*, 68, *68*
Prints, Liberty, history of, 6–7

Rosette trimmed tieback, 10
Ruffle, dust, *see* Valance
Ruffles, 142

Running stitch, 140

Salazar (print), *36*, 38
Santana (print), 14, 44, 46
Scherzo (print), 68
Scott, Jane, 17
Scott, Jerry, 17
Seams, 140
Seat covers, *see* Covers, seat
Sewing techniques
basting/tacking, 139
bias strips, 140
buttonhole, 139
fastenings, zip, 141
gathering stitch, 140
hemming, 139
ladderstitch, 139–140
lockstitch, 140
mitred corner, 141
folding, double hem, 141
single hem, 141
trimming, 141
oversewing, 140
piping, 141
prickstitch, 140
ruffles, double, 142
knife pleat, 142
single, 142
running (gathering) stitch, 140
seams, flat fell, 140
French, 140
slip knot, 142
slipstitch, 140
tacking/basting, 139
velcro, 142
zip fastening, 141
Silver, Arthur, 42
Silver, Harry, 7
Silver, Rex, 7
Smocked stool cover, 77, 137
tieback, 77, 107
Stewart-Liberty, Catherine, 9, 10
Stewart-Liberty, Liz, 33, 34
Stewart-Liberty, Oliver, 9
Stölzl, Gunta, 78
Stool cover, smocked, 77, 137
Studio, 66, 68
Suki (print), 58, 59, 60, 90, 91
Swags and tails, for bay window, 59, 60, 102
Sweet Pea (print), 26, *26*, 28,

28, 55, *55*
Sykes, Victoria, 26

Tablecloths, rectangular, 21, 124–5
round, fitted, with gathered skirt piping and double ruffle, 10, 124
with bound and headed ruffle, 14, 124
with bound edge, 44, 46, 123
vinyl coated, 79, 123
Tacking/basting, 139
Tambourine (print), 49
Tana lawns, *see* Collections
Tee, Susanna, 76
Terrace (print), 74
Tiebacks, bow, with contrast lining and edging, 10, 107
lined, with cord and contrast edging, 34, *34*, 107–8
measuring up, 106
ruffled, casing metal arm, 55, 56, 106–7
shaped, interlined with optional piping and rosette, *51*, 52, 60, 109
smocked, 77, 107
stiffened, with edging and rosette, 10, *10*, 108
Trent (print), 10

Valances (dust ruffle)
combined with curtain, 34, *34*, 100
curved, with ruffled piped edge, 24, 100
ruffled, 74, 129
split, with contrast bordered top, 18, 26, 28, 129–130
Velcro, 142
Victorian house, East Grinstead, 40–42
Voysey, C F A, 7

Walls, fabric, gathered, 72, 133–4
Webb, Philip, 40, *41*
Wilcock, Arthur, 7
Willshaw, Arthur, 7
Wilson, Peter, 44, 48
Winterbottom, Dudley and Mirjana, 51

ACKNOWLEDGEMENTS

The author and publishers would like to thank the following people for their help in the preparation of this book:
Algonquin Hotel, New York; Clement Freud; Valerie Goad; David Haward; Fred and Sarah Hohler; Island Cruising Club; James and Ingrid Kempston; Elina Labourdette; Paul Müller; The National Trust; Geoffrey Phillips, Liberty of London, New York; Mrs Raeburn; Mr and Mrs Rennoldson; Amanda Rowe; Paul Ruddock; Jerry and Jane Scott; Sue Scott; Catherine Stewart-Liberty; Liz Stewart-Liberty; Victoria Sykes; Bridget Watker; Dudley and Mirjana Winterbottom.

Photograph on page 21 by Pascal Hinous/Agence Top. The furniture featured on page 41 is not on permanent display at Standen, but was chosen to suit the period of the house.

The studio on page 67 was designed by Christine McCarron, Kaufmann Ford McCarron Ltd, 94 Belsize Lane, London NW3.

Photograph on page 79 supplied with kind permission by Ideal Home.